ITALIAN BATTLE FLEET 1940–43

'La Squadra', the pride of the Regia Marina

Enrico Cernuschi

Illustrated by Edouard A. Groult

OSPREY PUBLISHING
Bloomsbury Publishing Plc
Kemp House, Chawley Park, Cumnor Hill, Oxford OX2 9PH, UK
29 Earlsfort Terrace, Dublin 2, Ireland
1385 Broadway, 5th Floor, New York, NY 10018, USA
E-mail: info@ospreypublishing.com
www.ospreypublishing.com

OSPREY is a trademark of Osprey Publishing Ltd

First published in Great Britain in 2024

A catalogue record for this book is available from the British Library.

ISBN: PB 9781472860590; eBook 9781472860606; ePDF 9781472860576; XML 9781472860583

24 25 26 27 28 10 9 8 7 6 5 4 3 2 1

Maps by bounford.com
Diagrams by Adam Tooby
Index by Fionbar Lyons
Typeset by PDQ
Printed and bound in India by Replika Press Private Ltd.

Author's Note
Most British histories about the naval conflict fought in the Mediterranean during World War II
raise serious doubts about some of its central beliefs and strategies. After 1945, many English-speaking
secondary sources limited themselves to copying and pasting old wartime pamphlets, producing books
and articles which have set the general standards of the field; yet failed to make use of translations of
Italian original documents like the fundamental *Diari di Supermarina* (the Italian Navy Central
Command daily records). The conventional picture presented is therefore, unavoidably, misleading.
Research into unpublished sources such as the original warships' proceedings and logs – British,
Australian and Italian – allows us to understand differing perspectives of the same episodes which can
explain some of the unresolved issues.
It is natural that old adversaries saw things differently during and after the battle. Anyone can
legitimately think certain things are important and others are not, but details of a narrative can
transform the outcome of an event and, today, there is no excuse for ignoring historical evidence, on
either side.
As the ancient Greek historian and geographer Herodotus wryly concluded: 'It seems indeed to be
easier to deceive a multitude than one man'. The reader is that man.

Front Cover: Art by Edouard A. Groult, © Osprey Publishing
Osprey Publishing supports the Woodland Trust, the UK's leading woodland conservation charity.

To find out more about our authors and books visit www.ospreypublishing.com. Here you will find
extracts, author interviews, details of forthcoming events and the option to sign up for our newsletter.

Glossary of terms

CoS	Chief of Staff
	Decima Flottiglia MAS (also known as *La Decima* or *X MAS*)
MAS	*Motoscafo Anti Sommergibili* (a small MTB)
MGBs	Motor Gun Boats
MTBs	Motor Torpedo Boats
MMS	Motor Mine Sweepers
PTs	Patrol Torpedo boats

CONTENTS

THE FLEET'S PURPOSE

In 1914, the French Marine Nationale (MN), the Italian Regia Marina (RM) and the Austro-Hungarian k.(u.)k. Kriegsmarine were the three regional navies of the Mediterranean. All were unable, however, to project sea power beyond the Mediterranean except for a few armoured or protected cruisers and sloops. They also could not count on the most recent types of warships (super-dreadnoughts, battlecruisers and light cruisers) and technology (such as analogue mechanical fire-control instruments) that the advanced blue-water navies of Britain, Germany and the United States relied upon.

By 1919, the Habsburgs' navy had gone, and the French and Italian fleets were still some steps behind the Royal Navy (RN) and the US Navy (USN). The first fire-control systems were soon to be introduced, but there was still a long way to go to perfect them (although the Italian solution was more promising than the Vickers *conjugateur graphique* bought by the Marine Nationale after World War I). The MN's fleet included pseudo-super-dreadnoughts of the Bretagne class which were essentially Courbet-class dreadnoughts but with 13.39in guns. These offered only a 15,800yds range and the same thin armour as their predecessors. Italian big guns could, however, since 1916, reach 26,200yds, but their 12in main guns were unable to pierce the super-dreadnoughts' armoured decks (even by plunging fire from 9,000yds, as the Battle of Jutland had shown).

The real problem, however, for both Paris and Rome was the fact that the RN was now back in the Mediterranean after a long absence. In 1904, Britain's Mediterranean Fleet, not counting the squadron based at Gibraltar, wielded 12 pre-dreadnoughts. In 1914, this force had been reduced, due to the increasing German threat, to just three battlecruisers. France and Italy took advantage of Britain's changing priorities in 1911–12, pocketing Morocco, Libya and the Dodecanese islands in the Aegean Sea. During the post-war era, the 1st Battle Squadron based at Malta never had less than four modern battleships supported by a seaplane carrier (replaced from 1924, by a real aircraft carrier). The balance of power east of the Rock had changed. With the absence of Germany and Russia after their defeats, the Mediterranean appeared to expect a new *Pax Britannica*, crowding out the Latin powers' competing ambitions in the Middle East and the Balkans. Aside from this, the United States, in spite of their 1919-onwards policy advocating non-involvement in European and Asian conflicts, were far from satisfied by the Anglo-American convention regarding American rights in Palestine signed in 1924, and even less, in 1928, by the Red Line Agreement about oil monopolies in the ex-Ottoman territories.

Eastern Mediterranean, 1 September 1940. 15in Turrets 1 and 2 (A and B in the RN) of the R.N. (*Regia Nave* or Royal Warship) *Vittorio Veneto*. The modern 35,000t battleships of the Littorio class were the pride of the RM battleforce ('La Squadra', as it was called in Italy). They were the only real Italian battleships as the modernized dreadnoughts with their 12.6in guns lacked the power of the 15in guns. (AC)

This was the scenario into which the RM battleforce, the core of the Italian Navy, which had rejected journalistic ideas of a navy formed of submarines, aircraft and large 120-ton MTBs armed with 4in guns, would play its political and strategic role during the following quarter of a century.

After the 1918 disappearance of the five-century-old Austrian threat, Italy was able to pursue its economic interests and ambitions along all the Mediterranean coasts and beyond, on a much larger scale than before 1914. Theoretically, France was Rome's main adversary, as was the case between 1871 and 1914, but since 1919, Paris preferred to adopt a conciliatory policy towards Italy, while Britain was less cooperative.

During World War I, Italy and the 'Entente' (the UK, France and Russia) had been allies, not friends. Rome had been 'kindly blackmailed' to join the war by the British and French naval blockade, initiated from August 1914, however, by May 1915, 25 per cent of Italian factories had closed down because of lack of coal and raw materials. The partnership that followed between the respective navies was marked (like the Axis naval collaboration during World War II) by great formal courtesy and a general feeling of mistrust.

The tactical results of the Battle of Jutland were received with a certain satisfaction in Italy (and in France), as confirmation that 'Nelson's touch' was, after a century, a one-off. During the two main surface actions fought in the Adriatic on 29 December 1915 and 15 May 1917, the allied British and Italians pointed accusing fingers at each other, especially during the Action of the Strait of Otranto, when Admiral Alfredo Acton (later Chief of Staff of the RM, 1919–21 and 1925–27) was unimpressed by the Royal Navy, observing, after the light cruiser *Dartmouth* was struck by one 3.9in shell (judged, then and

Admiral Giuseppe Fioravanzo, the most important Italian strategist of the 20th century. In 1924, he authored the future strategy for the RM's naval conflict against the UK. During World War II, he alternated time at the Supermarina in 1940–42 with the command of the modern 35,000t battleships squadron and an autonomous cruiser squadron. As commander at Taranto, he had a clear-minded, decisive role in the directing of the Italian Navy during the Armistice and was ostensibly the real leader in Southern Italy as all public services were led or directly manned by the RM after the political and organizational collapse on 9 September 1943. He also broadcast to the public during 1940–43 about the ongoing naval situation. (AC)

later, by the British to be a 6in projectile), that the ship turned away at once, ordering her forward magazine to be flooded, and breaking off the pursuit of the Austro-Hungarian squadron.

Despite France's irritation with the Washington Naval Conference (1921–22), which ended by dictating a parity in French and Italian battleships, Paris and Rome agreed not to support Britain during the Turkish Chanak Crisis in 1922, contributing to Lloyd George's fall from power. A few days later, a new government in Rome led by Benito Mussolini complicated things even more.

The first big problem was the Corfu Incident in August 1923, when the RM bombarded and occupied the Greek island after the assassination of Italian officers near the Albanian border in Epirus. Britain had supported Athens since 1919 in the Balkans and Anatolia, in contrast to France, Italy and the United States. Mussolini believed that if the RM intervened, it would be possible to obtain consent for Italy to create a naval base in the Dodecanese (a decision Britain opposed until 1925), and perhaps to pocket Corfu itself.

When the Italian Navy Minister Admiral Paolo Thaon di Revel and the CoS Admiral Gino Ducci discovered, with horror, that Britain had not been appeased beforehand, as the new Prime Minister had agreed would happen, and that Mussolini was merely a chancer compared to the clever, daring and lucky Cavour, they faced him down to avoid a clash with the Mediterranean Fleet. Mussolini's reply demonstrated a total ignorance of sea power; he really believed submarines, MAS boats (the Italian MTBs) and aircraft could confront British battleships. To conclude, he asked how long the RM and Italy could endure a fight against Britain. Thaon di Revel's terse answer was '72 hours'. Diplomacy and French help – since Mussolini had supported the Franco-Belgian occupation of the Rhineland in 1923 – defused the crisis within a month with a settlement which required a formal apology from Greece, the neutralization of Corfu and the payment of an indemnity, delivered to the victims of the RM's bombardment of the ancient Venetian fortress at Corfu.

DOCTRINE

When Italy joined the Triple Alliance with Germany and Austria-Hungary, in 1882, Rome included a clause, the so-called *Lodo Mancini*, stating that on no account would the new kingdom fight a war against Britain, the naval superpower of the 19th century. In 1924–25, while Britain and Italy were agitating one another in the Middle and Far East, the RM considered, for the first time, the 'impossible hypothesis' of a conflict with Britain. The author of the strategy was brilliant Lieutenant Giuseppe Fioravanzo, who in 1921 had supported, the proposal for an Italian Navy 10,000t carrier.

The principles of his thinking were:

- Battleships (flanked by carriers) were the core of the navy. At the modern long ranges, the classic 5kt advantage requested since Tsushima to cross the T of the enemy line was not important, while armour was decisive.
- It would be very difficult to sink a modern battleship (not a battlecruiser) at the current and increasing ranges of naval artillery.
- Only very few direct hits would be obtained in these conditions. The USN estimated, in 1921, that its 16in guns would achieve, at 26,000yds, a 2 per cent success with the aid of efficient air spotting. Increased accuracy was possible as the distances decreased, but in such cases, the danger would be so great as to induce the force that was damaged first by the modern, huge ranges, to break off the engagement. The best long-range shooting battlefleet would thus gain local sea control, opening its sea lanes and closing them to the enemy.

In autumn 1916, the German submarine threat had induced British merchant shipping with the Empire to leave the Mediterranean and use the Cape Route as an alternative. But the year after, due to the by-now unrestricted U-boat warfare, this option had proved to be too expensive in terms of tonnage and home imports.

Pending the availability of modern battleships within the RM line of battle, if (a big if) Italy was able to induce the Mediterranean Fleet to leave its traditional and well-equipped base of Malta, then RM naval guerrilla strategy could close the Strait of Sicily to British commerce. Like the campaign against Austria-Hungary in the Upper Adriatic during World War I, this was planned to cause serious losses to the enemy and to threaten the Ionian Sea with mines and expendable warships, submarines and, at night, torpedo boats and a new type of large, 32t round-bilge MTB named 'autocannoniere'. The decisive tool for such a task had to be a railway battery based at Cape Passero, in the extreme southern corner of Sicily, consisting of 8.2in long-range siege guns based on some 15in guns manufactured during World War I for the four never-completed battleships of the Caracciolo class and modified as 210/102mm guns.

As history shows, Fioravanzo concluded proper use of sea power could facilitate victory, but the final success had to come by land. The local control of the central basin of the Mediterranean would therefore be exploited to ferry and supply, from Italy to Tobruk, a small *Regio Esercito* (Italian Army) motorized corps which had to cross the Western Desert to join the Egyptians, still troublesome after the revolt of 1919, and expel the small British garrison.

This ambitious programme was tested during the naval exercises of 1924–25, but no one, especially Mussolini, considered it probable. At the same time, the

Washington Treaty and budget constraints did not allow Italy (or France) to put on their slips anything bigger than heavy cruisers, while in 1927, the RN completed the 'two ugly sisters' *Nelson* and *Rodney* – the most powerful and heavily protected, and the only post-Jutland battleships in the world.

At the end of 1926, the balance of power in Europe was turned abruptly upside down as a clandestine quasi-war in the Balkans began, with the warring parties backed by France and Italy. Britain came down almost automatically on the side of Rome, which gave Italy some small economic and prestige satisfaction. The subsequent world crisis helped to avoid any naval race, confirming a substantive equality between the old RM and MN battleline and cruiser squadrons. In 1931, a further upheaval followed in Europe. The new French Prime Minister Pierre Laval, mesmerized by the by-now not-so-secret German rearmament, developed a new policy towards Italy, giving Mussolini a silent but ambiguous green light for his movements in East Africa. During the same year, the British adopted the Imperial Preference tariff, which promoted home production of goods over those of the Empire and foreign producers.

The global naval balance was affected again in 1931 by the French answer to the laying down in 1929 of the first German 10,000t pocket battleship, *Deutschland*. The new 26,500t warship, *Dunkerque*, begun in 1932, forced Italy to respond. Its budget did not allow, however, an order for any of the ambitious fast battleships from 28,000t to 35,000t planned by the RM between 1927 and 1933. The only option was a radical reconstruction, in 1933–37, of the old dreadnoughts *Cavour* and *Cesare*. In 1934, news about a fourth German warship of the Deutschland class followed by French parliamentary debates about the *Strasbourg*, a twin of *Dunkerque*, persuaded Mussolini (Minister of the Navy between 1925 and 1929 and, again, 1933–43), to follow his CoS Admiral Domenico Cavagnari's advice about the best choice of what to build: no half-measures like France, but the most powerful battleships in the world,

The modernized *Cavour* in 1937. A masterpiece of reconstruction designed by General GN Francesco Rotundi. The new machinery extended one full deck level higher than before, including a separate armour box to protect it using improved silicon-manganese ER Steel which seems to have been similar to the contemporary British D-Steel. (AC)

similar to the revolutionary Duilio class of 1871 which had downgraded other existing ironclads. Within a few months, these new 35,000t warships *Littorio* and *Vittorio Veneto* were laid down. The Admiralty and the British government did not believe the Italians would be able to complete them.

After Britain incorporated the region of Hadhramaut in South Arabia into the Empire in 1933 (without the approval of Paris and Rome), the British Colonial Office began a series of initiatives in Ethiopia which culminated (via the agreement about Zeila with Addis Ababa and the later Wal Wal Incident) in the Abyssinian Crisis of 1935–36. At that time, Italy still had only two fairly old dreadnoughts, *Doria* and *Duilio*, used to defend Augusta (Sicily) and Naples; while the RN, after leaving Malta in August 1935, had at least five battleships and two carriers in the Mediterranean. Cavagnari had adopted, since 1933, Fioravanzo's doctrine with a personal variant: tonnage war, and a powerful ally like France or, at worst, Germany, would suffice.

The Italian Army's long-range gun had proved a failure in 1935, however, the Regia Aeronautica (RA), the Italian Air Force, had long been vocal in promoting propaganda about its speed records and transatlantic flights (particularly since the arrival of future Air Marshal Italo Balbo); this propaganda proved extremely effective, and the RN relinquished nearby Malta in August 1935 for the almost non-existent naval base of Alexandria and the modest facilities of Gibraltar.

The Abyssinian Crisis in 1936 was immediately followed by the unexpected Spanish Civil War. Considering it to be something of a 20th-century War of the Spanish Succession, Britain did not obstruct the Italian intervention into Spain, confident that Mussolini would never try to annex the Balearic Islands or anything else. However, after the abdication of King Edward VIII, a friend of the Italian monarch Victor Emmanuel III since 1916, the British attitude underwent a sharp change and the clandestine RM surface and submarine campaigns against Republican Spanish shipping in 1936–37 were studded with incidents where RN warships were attacked. This did not improve Italian–British relations. In September 1937, the British Admiralty was charged, for the first time since 1912, with planning for a brief naval war against Italy. Almost simultaneously, two modernized Cavours were commissioned. The RM had at last a small, modern battle squadron.

The path to war and the development of the Axis relationship in 1936–39 was a predictable evolution. When war began in summer 1940, the RM had to face the RN with a battleship force conceived in 1932 to face France only. Italy's plans had never envisaged a war against the UK, but just a confrontation as had happened in Ethiopia in 1935, which would reshuffle the cards in the Middle East and the Balkans and lead to a peace conference to overturn the Versailles settlement. The decision for a new pair of Littorios was made in December 1937, with the new battleships *Roma* and *Impero* scheduled to enter service in late 1941.

FLEET FIGHTING POWER

THE SHIPS
The Mediterranean after World War I

During World War II, Italy's battlefleet was formed by battleships (a category including both the so-called super-dreadnoughts, dreadnoughts and the surviving battlecruisers of World War I), cruisers and fleet destroyers. In 1919, the RM had five dreadnoughts in service: *Dante Alighieri*, the twins *Conte di Cavour* and *Giulio Cesare*, and their half-sisters *Andrea Doria* and *Duilio*. At the same time, the French Navy battle line was formed by the dreadnoughts *Courbet*, *France*, *Jean Bart* and *Paris*, and by the super-dreadnoughts (or almost) *Bretagne*, *Provence* and *Lorraine*.

On the slips there were, respectively, four battleships of Italy's Caracciolo class and five of France's Normandie class, but there was no chance they would be completed as their design had been compromised by the Battle of Jutland. Too thinly protected, they lacked an adequate armoured deck against long-range plunging projectiles, which the dreadnoughts' single-calibre big-gun main armament and modern fire-control directors now made possible.

A study was completed in 1917 examining a reconstruction of *Caracciolo*, to improve the original horizontal armoured deck of only 2in (actually 30 + 14mm, i.e. much less than the 2½–1in decks of RN battlecruisers lost at Jutland), to a new 90–110mm deck (3.54–4.33in), but this implied an increase in the ships' draught and displacement (to 34,000t), which compromised the effectiveness of the side belt. The idea was dropped and, in 1919, the Ansaldo yard of Genoa proposed, as a private venture, to use *Caracciolo*'s hull and machinery for a conversion to an aircraft carrier (following the lines of the British *Argus*) or as a fast seaplane carrier. The idea was refused by the Navy for budgetary reasons and the ship, launched in 1920, was sold to a cruise line. The prospect of converting *Caracciolo* to a merchant vessel was soon relinquished as, after a revision of the programme, it was considered too expensive. The hull was towed to Baia, near

Naples, in December 1920 and mothballed there, at the expense of the RM, in view of a possible emergency conversion to a carrier.

The full picture of the dreadnought situation in the Mediterranean during those years also includes the former Austro-Hungarian battleships *Prinz Eugen* and *Tegetthoff*, seized by the RM in November 1918 at Pola. The first was handed to the French in 1919 who sank her as a target on 22 June 1922, according to the terms of the peace treaty. The Italians cheated, preserving the *Tegetthoff* in Venice until late 1923 when the battleship was sent to La Spezia to be broken up gradually over the next two years.

A proposal was made, in November 1919, to recover the capsized Austro-Hungarian *Viribus Unitis*, sunk at dawn on 1 November 1918 by an Italian attack craft, from the sea bottom – thus circumventing the rules of the peace treaty signed at Versailles. This plan was soon abandoned and the battleship was broken and recovered piecemeal during the 1920s.

In 1921, the threat of an enduring first rate naval power in the Adriatic Sea after the end of Austria-Hungary, vanished. Belgrade had planned to buy (with Czechoslovakian money) the former White Russian battleship *General Alekseev*, just interned at Bizerte, and some large and modern destroyers with a seaplane carrier. The programme was rejected, wisely, by Paris to avoid any complication with Rome and the warships soon become, because of lack of maintenance, scrap iron.

Naval Aviation Struggles

In 1921, the RM asked for a 7,000t fast seaplane carrier and two non-protected and fast 5,000t cruisers armed with eight 6in high-velocity guns (152mm/50). These had been designed in 1914 following the new Italian naval ballistic doctrine envisaged in 1909. According to the original schedule of 1913, this new gunnery system would become viable during the 1920s once the necessary Italian-made rangefinders and fire-control calculating machines were completed and tested. The Caracciolos, conceived in 1910, were, in fact, a stop-gap solution, with their originally planned 12 15in guns[1] whose range was limited to 19,600yds, to face the announced (and never laid down) four Austro-Hungarian Ersatz Monarch-class battleships, armed with ten 13.8in guns, 21kt and a displacement of 24,500t.

18 March 1937 Tripoli. Mussolini, Balbo, the party secretary Achille Starace and Minister Alessandro Lessona on the cruiser *Pola*. Behind them Admiral Cavagnari, the often-ignored naval adviser of Il Duce between 1933 and 1940. (AC)

---

1 *Caracciolo* carried eight main guns in the final version, displacing 31,400t with a 28kt top speed.

The 1920s budget crisis caused by wartime debts to Britain (the richer United States, by far the biggest lender to Italy's balance of payments, had since 1919 granted very generous conditions, while France was almost absent from Rome's general ledger) caused the cancellation of the two cruisers until 1926, when they were finally ordered. It took another two years for them to be laid down – still because of lack of funds – following a new and much-debated design proposed in 1924 by Colonel Genio Navale (GN: Naval Engineering Corps) Giuseppe Rota. The fast seaplane carrier too was a victim of the Treasury axe. In August 1922, the final, weak, parliamentary Liberal government before Mussolini decided to end its construction. It preferred a cheaper option: converting a passenger ship on the slip which became the *Giuseppe Miraglia*, a 4.880t, 21kt vessel with two catapults, carrying a dozen floatplanes or small flying boats. She was only marginally stable, so much so that she capsized in 1925 before being completed. *Miraglia* was recovered and commissioned two years later.[2]

When the modernization of the two Cavours was finally confirmed in 1932, after a year of doubts, *Miraglia* would be too slow to steam with the future battleships. The adoption in 1933 of two bulges to increase stability made her even slower, too slow for anything other than auxiliary tasks as a transport and depot ship. The final bill was more than the original 7,000t true warship planned in 1920 would have cost – a waste of money. The availability of a fast seaplane carrier with about ten floatplanes would have addressed what was the biggest handicap suffered by the World War II RM by day: insufficient air reconnaissance.

The real tragedy for the RM was, however, the introduction, in 1923, of the Regia Aeronautica (RA), the Italian Air Force. The new service had been strongly advocated by some of the most efficient blackshirt leaders, themselves Army demobilized aviators. Always a Lilliputian force (with an average of about 1,200 fighters, attack aircraft and reconnaissance planes during World War II, facing more than 5,000 in the RAF or the Luftwaffe), the RA was always concerned about a rebirth of the Forza Aerea, the Italian naval air branch incorporated in 1923 (similar to when the RAF absorbed the Royal Naval Air Service between April 1918 and May 1939, or the French Aéronavale was put at the orders of the Air Force between 1928 and 1932). Being *Il Duce*'s pet service, the RA starkly opposed any Navy proposal that appeared to intrude on its territory. No carriers, no torpedo bombers, no (from 1931) bombers or fighters controlled by the RM; only some air reconnaissance groups (MARINAVIA) formed by floatplanes and flying boats based on land, and spotters on the warships with Navy officers as observers, but not pilots.

The number of reconnaissance aircraft and their type were, in any case, decided by the RA, and its available strength before and during World War II

---

2 At the same time, France commissioned the experimental carrier *Béarn*, which had been laid down as a battleship of the Normandie class. Converted with British help, *Béarn* had similarly little success, being slow (21kt) and with little stability; the carrier's first reliable torpedo bombers were embarked only in 1930.

(less than 200 aircraft) would always be half of the size planned in 1931 for a war against France alone.

An idea about reconstructing the dreadnought *Leonardo da Vinci* as a carrier (sunk by an internal explosion in 1916, refloated upside down in 1919 and righted two years later) was short-lived during 1922, as her hull was considered inappropriate for such a role. A 10,180t carrier for 20 aircraft was planned in 1923, but the RA stopped construction the next year, not only because of budgetary constraints. The design, made by the OTO (Odero-Terni-Orlando) yard of Livorno, was proposed later, in a slightly reduced version, by the affiliate CRDA-Trieste company to Argentina as an alternative to a third cruiser for the Veinticinco de Mayo class built in Italy by OTO, but the programme for a third warship was cancelled by Buenos Aires in 1928 both for budgetary and political reasons.

The seaplane carrier *Giuseppe Miraglia*. A very short-lived capital ship. During World War II, she served as a depot ship for floatplanes and submarines and for the trials of the Re.2000 fighters embarked, from September 1942, on the Littorios. (AC)

In 1924, the Italian government had declared itself unable to pay for new cruisers and a carrier. In August 1925, the RM admirals instead asked for a pair of 12,480t, 34kt, heavy cruiser-carrier hybrids, armed with eight 8in guns in two quadruple turrets, and designed by Colonel GN Rota. Mussolini's answer was that the money was not there and this idea too was dropped. Minister of the Navy Thaon di Revel, while complaining about the law which only gave the Army (Italy's 'Senior Service') the role of Chief of the General Staff,[3] had declared to Parliament that a 10,000t carrier would be too vulnerable under the waterline and that it would be necessary to order a 25–30,000t ship (in essence the *Caracciolo*). Di Revel resigned in May 1925, and in 1926 the newly appointed RA Secretary Italo Balbo persuaded Mussolini to scrap the *Caracciolo* hull.

In December 1927, a further proposal for an experimental carrier of slightly less than 10,000t (a new design by Colonel GN Curio De Bernardis, which would allow Italy to commission a carrier without touching the total tonnage terms of the Washington Naval Treaty) was requested by the deputy CoS of the Navy, Rear-Admiral Romeo Bernotti. But the proposal was repulsed by Balbo and Mussolini. The RM obtained, on the same occasion, the green light for a four-year programme which included the four heavy cruisers of the Zara class and a third Trento, the *Bolzano*, being therefore able to even the score with the French 8in cruisers now authorized in Paris (*Suffren*, *Colbert* and *Foch*) or envisaged (*Dupleix* and *Algérie*). Due to lack of funds, neither France nor Italy

---

3 The Italian Navy only obtained this prerogative in 1972.

had taken advantage of the clause of the treaty signed in Washington in 1922, which had allowed them to build new battleships since 1927.

In addition, by 1928, the battleship *Dante* had been paid off. Two years later, the three too-old, too-slow Courbets were transformed into gunnery and signal training ships. A series of studies were made, together with a design scheduled for 1931 by General GN Filippo Bonfiglietti, for a 15,000t, 29kt light carrier. This programme too was vehemently opposed by Balbo, with Mussolini's ideological approval, in spite of the fact that the RM had saved, year after year, money for a first ship. In 1932, a new proposal was made. This time it was a design by General GN Giuseppe Vian for two small 10,000t aircraft carriers which could be built by the minor Italian yards leaving free, for any emergencies, the only two Italian shipyards which were more than 200m (218yds) long, and adequately equipped with heavy cranes: Ansaldo-Genoa and CRDA-Trieste, both modernized between 1928 and 1930, to build the new 50,000gwt superliners *Rex* and *Conte di Savoia*.

This idea was scuttled too and the money saved by the RM was transferred to the Army-controlled General Staff, which used it to buy an 'untouchable reserve' of cast iron at its disposal only. The amazed Germans discovered it intact after the Italian armistice was announced on 8 September 1943. This was the last missed opportunity for an Italian carrier during World War II.

A possible Italian carrier sideshow was the Portuguese deal for a seaplane carrier to be named *Sacadura Cabral*. The design, proposed by OTO in 1930, was for a 6,096t warship, 22kt, with four 4.7in guns and 12 floatplanes. Like other orders assigned by Lisbon to OTO, the warship too was deferred after the 1931 devaluation of sterling and, in the end, cancelled in 1934.

A last effort was made between 1932 and 1933, when the RM, after the Vian design for a carrier was abandoned, studied a successor for the *Miraglia*. The idea was to build a 5,000t, 27kt cruiser armed with two 6in triple turrets and three catapults, one fixed on the forecastle and two, revolving, aft. The ship would have been able to serve in East Africa as a submarine depot ship and would have been equipped with five floatplanes. The idea was discarded at the end of 1933, by the new Secretary of the Navy, Cavagnari, hostile to any compromise on the path of the long-awaited aircraft carrier.

Surface Fleet Rearmament

Until 1931, the naval parity between Italy and France had remained balanced. In 1922, the MN ordered three unprotected cruisers of the Duguay-Trouin class and, later, three further minor and one-offs (*Pluton*, *Jeanne d'Arc* and *Émile Bertin*). Italy replied in 1926–28 with six Condottieris. They too were unprotected, but budgetary restrictions and prestige needs resulted in a 5,000t design with the power (eight 6in guns) of a 7,200t Duguay-Trouin. The architectural solution found by Colonel GN Rota was to concentrate the main steam pipes in a single, vulnerable position with no redundancy. The high block coefficient of the little Condottieris' hulls caused hard rolling, interfering with their gunnery.

During the August 1925 meeting with Mussolini, the admirals informed the Prime Minister about this weakness, but the conclusion was that the likelihood of such damage to the pipes was low, and would be a case of extremely bad luck. However, this is exactly what did happen on 19 July 1940 when *Colleoni* was hit off Cape Spada.

The following generation of light cruisers ordered in 1931–32 were much more balanced. France's six La Galissoniére class were matched by Italy's four similar Montecuccoli/Eugenio di Savoia class, and followed by the two bigger Abruzzi class. These cruisers now had adequate protection in which a totally new electric system with triple redundancy served the rudder, fire-control, searchlights, the telephone lines and the various services needing AC (including weapons). Warships' electrical power had increased from 39kW on the 670-ton three-stacker destroyer *Sirtori* in 1917 to 6,800kW on *Vittorio Veneto* 20 years later. During the war, the battleships were modified with further emergency cables inside the cofferdams. Wartime experience confirmed this as a weakness of the first generation of Italian cruisers: *Pola* and *Trento* were immobilized and later lost, respectively in March 1941 and June 1942, after being hit by a torpedo and losing all electric power. In comparison, the durability of the second generation was demonstrated in similar incidents, by *Garibaldi* in July 1941 and *Abruzzi* four months later. It is necessary to add, however, that there were episodes (*Bolzano* in August 1941 and *Trieste* in November 1941) when torpedoes hit older vessels, but the electric generating sets worked by the book, saving the ship.

As previously mentioned, the 1930s saw a fierce battleship competition between the RM and the MN. In 1931–32, *Dunkerque* was laid down, and the rebuilding of *Conte di Cavour* and *Giulio Cesare* was ordered; in 1934, *Strasbourg*, *Littorio* and *Vittorio Veneto* (known to sailors as *Veneto*) were all ordered.

Taranto, 1 November 1940. *Vittorio Veneto* sailors saluting Mussolini, standing on the motorboat running between the battleship and a destroyer. In tribute to the Italian Parallel War principle, i.e. a war alongside Germany, but not for Germany, the victory against Austria-Hungary in 1918 was always celebrated until spring 1943 in spite of German annoyance. (AC)

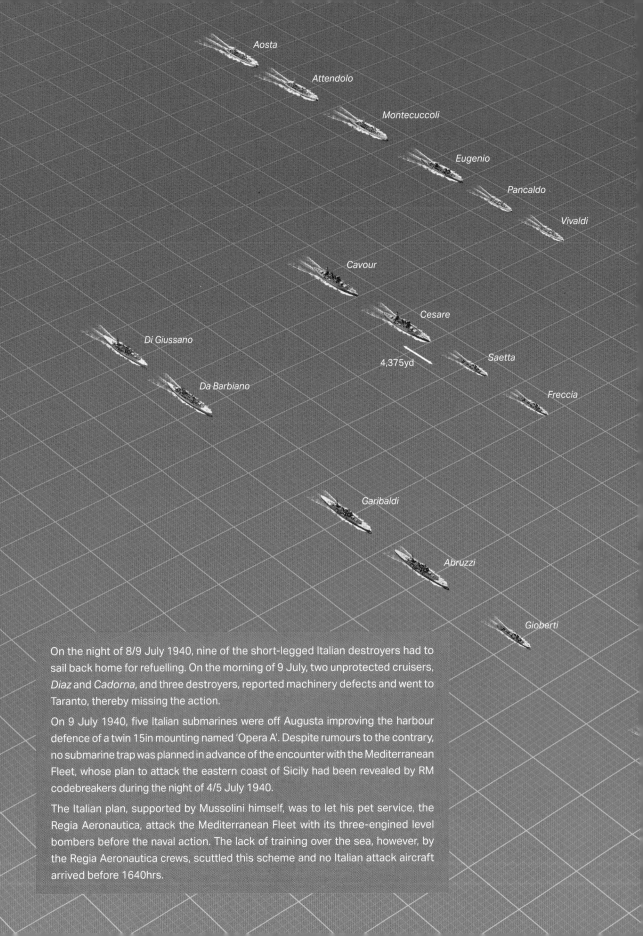

Aosta

Attendolo

Montecuccoli

Eugenio

Pancaldo

Vivaldi

Cavour

Cesare

Di Giussano

4,375yd

Saetta

Da Barbiano

Freccia

Garibaldi

Abruzzi

Gioberti

On the night of 8/9 July 1940, nine of the short-legged Italian destroyers had to sail back home for refuelling. On the morning of 9 July, two unprotected cruisers, *Diaz* and *Cadorna*, and three destroyers, reported machinery defects and went to Taranto, thereby missing the action.

On 9 July 1940, five Italian submarines were off Augusta improving the harbour defence of a twin 15in mounting named 'Opera A'. Despite rumours to the contrary, no submarine trap was planned in advance of the encounter with the Mediterranean Fleet, whose plan to attack the eastern coast of Sicily had been revealed by RM codebreakers during the night of 4/5 July 1940.

The Italian plan, supported by Mussolini himself, was to let his pet service, the Regia Aeronautica, attack the Mediterranean Fleet with its three-engined level bombers before the naval action. The lack of training over the sea, however, by the Regia Aeronautica crews, scuttled this scheme and no Italian attack aircraft arrived before 1640hrs.

LA SQUADRA BEFORE THE ACTION OFF CALABRIA

The Italian naval programmes mirrored the French ones until 1933. The RM consequently had an excess of cruisers, but lacked aircraft carriers and longer-range, bigger destroyers. During the Action off Calabria on 9 July 1940, the abundance of cruisers allowed Admiral Campioni to use a vanguard and a rearguard of, respectively, heavy and light cruisers with some extra as a scouting reserve force (VIII and IV Divisione). The objective was to engage RN battleships before they could form a line of battle. Campioni would then be able to position his squadron favourably to the sun and the wind and use his speed advantage to balance his lack of armour when confronting the British 15in guns. It was impossible to engage all Italian cruisers at once as an enemy vessel could only be the target of two warships. Both the Italian and British navies had low opinions about concentration fire.

Geniere

Trento

Aviere

Camicia Nera

Bolzano

Pola

Ascari

Artigliere

Zara

Corazziere

Gorizia

3,280yd

Carabiniere

Fiume

Lanciere

Carducci

Oriani

Alfieri

In 1935, France replied with the 35,000t battleships *Jean Bart* and *Richelieu*. But in truth, since 1931, Paris had not been considered a probable enemy in Rome. The German threat was the real problem for both France and Italy. As an act of goodwill, France transferred the three Bretagnes to the Atlantic Squadron in 1934. The following Anglo-German Naval Agreement, signed in London on 18 June 1935, allowed Berlin, without the advice of Britain's previous allies who were conveniently bypassed, to build a new fleet of 35 per cent of the Royal Navy's total tonnage, all of which did not help any entente along the two sides of the Channel. In turn, the Italians were worried about the Germans selling modern weapons, from 37mm anti-tank guns to small arms, to Ethiopia. When the MN proposed, in 1935, the conversion of the two heavy cruisers of the Duquesne class (by now considered too vulnerable as their protection was limited to gun-shields and a splinter-proof conning tower) into light carriers with a dozen aircraft, it was not an anti-Italian move (the RM being without carriers) but as a countermeasure against Britain.

When the chance of a war against Britain for Ethiopia became a real and present danger, Cavagnari went back to Mussolini to demand a carrier. After having dropped the proposal to rebuild the dreadnoughts *Doria* and *Duilio* as carriers in early 1935, the Italian admirals now asked for a speedy conversion, within 12 months, of the 32,582gwt liner *Roma* as an emergency carrier, along the lines of the future Allied escort carriers of World War II. Mussolini refused in October 1935, explaining that his opposition was based on economic and operative arguments: that the warship, with her original machinery built in 1914 for a Caracciolo-class battleship, would only be able to do 20kt.

Naples, May 1938. The large Italian submarine fleet was the best deterrent towards the RN during the four 1935–37 crises in the Mediterranean. Its value was considered much reduced by the British after the introduction of ASDIC from summer 1937. (AC)

As a result, in 1936, the RM proposed a new, more ambitious conversion by Colonel GN Luigi Gagnotto. This time the ship had to be similar to the British carrier *Furious*, and be capable of 26kt once new diesel engines were fitted; these had been recently proposed by the FIAT enterprise for the planned modernization of the liner *Roma* and her step-sister *Augustus*. The delayed manufacture of these new 7,100bhp engines (the most powerful in the world), which only made their final, successful trial in autumn 1942, defeated this plan too.

23 February 1942. The sinking, by a Cant Z 501 flying boat and the torpedo boat *Circe*, of the British submarine P 38. Italian ASW doctrine and effectiveness evolved together with the RN underwater campaign during 1940–43. Forty nine British or Allied boats were lost in the Mediterranean Sea before 8 September 1943. (AC)

In 1936, Cavagnari proposed to Mussolini, in the wake of the conquest of Addis Ababa, a hugely ambitious ten-year naval programme for a gigantic breakout fleet formed (including the former programmes now completed or in progress) of nine battleships, three carriers, 36 cruisers, 142 destroyers and torpedo boats, 84 submarines, 16 sloops, 24 submarine hunters and much else. A Plan B proposal was for six battleships, 22 cruisers and 116 destroyers and torpedo boats.

The Italian Navy had, in 1936, two old dreadnoughts (and four more being modernized or under construction, in the yards of Genoa and Trieste), 21 cruisers (and two others on the slips) and 135 destroyers and torpedo boats, old warships included. Plan B was, thus, only a modernization programme. Among the battleships of this last programme, there were two which were a sort of Italian 17,500t pocket battleship, diesel-engined and with a main armament of six 10in guns.

It was, anyway, a pipe dream as the Italian budget, after the strain of the economic sanctions voted by the League of Nations and enforced in 1935–36, had no chance of making this materialize. Much cheaper and more promising were the new generation of attack craft studied and tested from 1935: SLC (*Siluro a Lenta Corsa*), the so-called human torpedo, nicknamed '*maiale*' (pig) by the crews as its sailing qualities were simply terrible; MAT (*Motoscafi Aviotrasportati da Turismo*) explosive motor boats; and 'frogman' combat divers.

After the successes of World War I, a new generation of small attack craft had been tested during the 1920s, from radio-controlled MAS boats to a very fast 8t motor torpedo boat of Austro-Hungarian origin, designed to enter enemy harbours, whose prototype had been found almost ready at Pola in November 1918. They were all failures, but Cavagnari[4] supported any idea for a third generation of attack craft, despite the immediate refusal by the Italian Air Force to supply the S 55 floatplanes which had, according to the

---

4   Cavagnari was himself a commander who, in 1916, distinguished himself by entering the Channel of Fasana in Istria at night, with his torpedo boat towing a MAS, forcing the boom defence.

Taranto, 12 November 1940. The battleship *Littorio* stranded. She was hit by three torpedoes and repaired by 19 March 1941, sorting from the drydock and beginning a two-month retraining of her crew. (AC)

original programmes, to be used to ferry the new secret weapons near the British bases of Alexandria and Gibraltar. The special craft were, from the beginning, not a substitute for battleships, but a long-range weapon system to be used beyond the range of the battleforce.

In August 1936, Italy had the option to order a 13,000t carrier designed by General GN Umberto Pugliese, with new sandwich underwater protection replacing his previous longitudinal drum system, devised in 1917 and tested successfully by the tanker *Brennero* four years later. Mussolini again stubbornly refused to order the carrier, and instead the two Richelieus (by now the future core of a no-longer-friendly France) would be answered with the reconstruction, ordered in 1936 and begun the next year, of the dreadnoughts *Duilio* and *Doria*. They would be no match for the future MN battleships, but for lack of a better alternative, they could be useful as they were equipped with the same, very advanced fire-direction as the Littorios.

To escort its capital ships, the RM had never more than about 40 destroyers at a time, varying between the two categories of '*cacciatorpediniere*' and '*esploratori leggeri*', united under the same classification in 1938. The '*Tre pipe*' (three-stackers) of World War I and the two-funnel ships of the early 1920s were rated as torpedo boats and assigned to coastal command duties.

The light carrier programme was proposed again in 1937, 1938 and 1939, unsuccessfully, due to the renewed opposition from Mussolini and the RA. Instead, in December 1937, two improved Littorios, *Roma* and *Impero*, were ordered. This time the idea was to get eight battleships (four Littorios and four modernized ones) for 1942, in the expectation of a showdown with Britain and France to redraw the maps of the Middle East and the Balkans after '*una grande conferenza per la pace*' (a great conference for peace) with the support of its new German partner. France replied in 1938 with orders for two further 35,000t battleships, *Clemenceau* and *Gascogne*, and two 18,000t carriers, *Joffre* and *Painlevé*. *Painlevé* and *Gascogne* were never begun. On the other side of the Alps, France's yards and naval industries were in a much poorer state than Italy's, and *Richelieu* and *Jean Bart* were not yet completed when the new Prime Minister Marshal Pétain had to ask for an armistice in June 1940, with *Clemenceau* and *Joffre* not even launched.

Now was no longer the time for a confrontation in the Mediterranean with the French Third Republic but instead for a war against the much tougher and impregnable Britain.

TECHNICAL FACTORS

Italian naval machinery had high fuel consumption, but proved to be powerful and reliable, and Italian warship designers were competent and original. Between the two world wars, Italian warship exports were second, by a fraction, only to the British.

Italy's homogeneous armour, called AOC, was, according to tests undertaken in the USA after the war using plates from *Impero*, roughly on a par with the USN 'B' armour (in itself superior, in the thicker plates, compared to Germany's famous new '*Wotan harte*' armour of the Bismarck class).

The four rebuilt battleships had deck protection over magazines and 2in spaced armour surrounding the barbettes, which assured a considerable improvement against medium- and long-range shell fire and armour-piercing (AP) bombs. The Littorios had armoured decks 6.38in over the magazines and 3.94in over the engine and boiler rooms. A world-first was their spaced decapping plates[5] on virtually all of their heavy vertical armour. One deficiency was that their main belt was, like the Nelsons, shallow below the waterline, which exposed them to successful underwater hits. Regarding the heavy cruisers, the British did not expect that their 6in shells could penetrate the Zaras' armour beyond 7,000yds while the Trentos had an immunity zone far off 24,000yds. The RN light cruisers except the Southamptons were all vulnerable to the 8in shells within an approximate area between 17,000 and 24,000yds.

The generation of hardened armour produced after World War I was around 30 per cent superior in resistance to the equivalent armour plates of 1914 and it was extremely difficult to sink a battleship by gunfire, with the relatively soft-skinned *Hood* being an exception. The chance of getting a very-long-range hit during an action was unlikely even with the improved fire-control systems of the 1930s, if, for no other reason, than the flight-time of the shell allowed the target to change course, and both sides used smoke and evasive manoeuvres to complicate the enemy's fire-control problem. Other variables were the size of the target, its speed and, of course, visibility. The RM stereoscopic rangefinders were considered superior to the RN coincidence types by the British, who considered the limit for accurate fire-control to be less than 30,000yds. Straddles that included no hits were common.

The general rule is that the bigger the gun, the greater the accuracy. As dispersion tends to be inversely proportional to calibre, the new, larger generation of artillery had higher muzzle velocities and better ballistic performance with longer ranges, a flatter trajectory and a shorter time of flight. Accordingly, the RM adopted a high-velocity/very-heavy projectile combination for good range and armour penetration. The RN had shells with almost identical properties, but a bigger bursting charge. In terms of their guns' charges (chemical stability and burning efficiency) the RM had,

---

5   Designed to knock the cap off an armour-piercing capped shell on impact, reducing its effectiveness.

An Italian 12.6in shell in the Venice Naval Museum. These AP shells (14lb of TNT) had strengthened casing and, thus, little space for the bursting charge, whose blast and fire effect was like a 10in projectile, something no longer used against battleships since the widespread introduction of homogeneous Krupp-type armour from 1905. After the Action off Calabria, the RN discovered, with dismay, that the Queen Elizabeth battleships were not immune, as previously believed, to Chance Vital Hits (C.V.H.) in the face of these plunging shells. (AC)

according to the study made by Kent R. Crawford and Nicholas W. Mitiukov, a slight primacy in comparison to the RN.

As the spread of shots in a salvo was random, only a minimal percentage of projectiles, averaged over many salvos, would actually hit. It was not by chance that the minimum spotting correction for the RN was 400yds and for the RM 437yds (400m). Near-miss detonations (within 30ft of the ship according to the RN's confidential pre-printed forms) were part of expected damage too, because they caused a powerful gas bubble expanding in the direction of least resistance through the hull plating below the bottom edge of the armour, causing structural damage. Big guns' heavy splinters could hit the ship up to 90yds away, riddling the superstructure, bridge and turrets, causing potentially considerable wreckage and casualties.

At war, the Italian Admirals Inigo Campioni and Angelo Iachino considered the RN gunnery: '*né ordinato né efficace, benché raggruppato*' ('neither ordered nor effective, even though with little spread'). A judgement confirmed, after the war, by all the RM's wartime reports about day actions and by the recollections of officers and sailors.

The RN high-shell expenditure compromised the final phase of the action off Cape Spada. In 1944, the RN discovered that its guns fired short of the distance fire-control officers were trained to achieve on the basis of their range tables.

The Italians noted from July 1940 that at long ranges the British 6in shells often did not explode and, during the war, many RN 6in which hit were duds. The only recorded Italian projectile which did not explode (after hitting HMS *Cairo* on 15 June 1942) was, actually, a Skoda-made 14cm shell whose base fuze was found defective.

As we will see in the Analysis chapter, the Italians' so-called excessive spread, quoted so often in Anglophone literature, in fact assured a considerable advantage in terms of 'danger space' compared to the British fairly tight patterns.

Anti-aircraft RM weapons were more effective than the British pom-poms and 0.5in MGs until 1942, when American-made 40mm Bofors and 20mm Oerlikon cannons were introduced. American intelligence considered the Breda 37/54 (1.457in) twin and single mountings, with a 125rpm per barrel rate of fire, a very effective light anti-aircraft gun and the Breda 20/65 heavy MG an excellent AA gun.

The RM torpedoes too (all classic wet-heaters with natural air and kerosene fuel) were considered by the British to have very high performance, and to be reliable and effective. Lack of electric torpedoes and magnetic pistols until late 1942, however, reduced their effectiveness against well-trained RN crews.

Like France, Russia and Japan, Italian technology lagged behind that of Britain, America and Germany in electronics, radar and sonar before and during World War II, due to the limited home market for technology, which delayed commercial research and development. In May 1942, the RM began to move from experimental to effective Italian radar sets, EC3 ter Gufo at sea and RDT 1 Folaga on the ground.

However, the real drawback was the lack of adequate air reconnaissance at sea, both in numbers and types of aircraft. The Sunderland, for example, did not have different, more powerful or better engines than the contemporary Italian ones. It was the RA which considered flying boats much more expensive than floatplanes, refusing, from late 1936, any proposals for equivalent planes like the four-engined Caproni Ca 403 flying boat, the Ca 406 designed by engineer Pegna, or the CMASA four-engined bomber and reconnaissance flying boat BS12 with retracting stabilizing floats in the outboard engine nacelles. The idea to increase the number of the squadriglie of MARINAVIA (another quite possible choice, with available personnel, raw materials and production capacities in excess) was, then, an anathema for the RA which was happy to disband the Navy-controlled command in 1944, restoring it only in 1956.

RADAR ADVANTAGE: THE NIGHT ACTION OFF CAPE MATAPAN (overleaf)

Admiral Cattaneo's I Divisione – cruisers Zara and Fiume and four destroyers – was sent by Iachino to tow the immobilized cruiser Pola despite Cattaneo's proposal to recover the crew with two destroyers and scuttle her. I Divisione had to do a Butakov pipe turn, being without radar, to find Pola in an almost moonless night but HMS Orion's radar had spotted the immobilized cruiser, and I Divisione's course was betrayed by the bright light of the planet Jupiter behind it. They were sighted visually at first by the British lookouts on the taller platforms of the Warspite, Valiant and Barham, and ambushed point-blank (3,000yds). In this illustration, Zara is being smashed with only a twin 37mm MG surviving port side. The Italian fleet claimed a small hit first on Barham, which turned through 360°, then on Valiant. According to the British press, H.R.H. Prince Philip, a midshipman on Valiant, 'survived unscathed amid his shattered lights as an enemy cannon shell ripped into his position'. The Duke later spoke of how he coped when his shipmates died or were wounded: 'It was part of the fortunes of war' he said. 'We didn't have counsellors rushing around every time somebody let off a gun, you know, asking "Are you all right – are you sure you don't have a ghastly problem?".' You just got on with it.'. According to Prince Philip, Valiant received 'another eight-foot hole, narrow but deep, in the starboard torpedo protection bulges amidships.' It was claimed by the destroyer Carducci with her first, and last, 4.7in shell salvo before she was hit by Valiant. In 1945, the Report of Med. Intelligence Centre confirmed: 'Our losses – a few hits by gunfire'. In 1977, Captain Roskill wrote, in his book, Churchill & the Admirals, that Lord Salisbury, Secretary of State for the Dominions, did not approve of the fact that the Admiralty had 'boasted that our Fleet did not receive a scratch' in the Night Action off Matapan.

HOW THE FLEET OPERATED

COMMAND AND COMMUNICATION

Action off Calabria, 9 July 1940. Admiral Inigo Campioni on *Cesare*. Appointed Governor of the Dodecanese in July 1941, he resisted the German aggression after 8 September 1943. Taken prisoner by the Germans, he was tried by a fascist court at Parma and shot on 24 May 1944. (AC)

Between 1914 and February 1917, the RM had suffered from a conflict about strategy between the battlefleet commander, the Duke of the Abruzzi, who was a cousin of the King and a believer in the 'great-decisive-naval-battle' (a myth the Austro-Hungarians were not going to oblige), and the two-times Navy CoS, Thaon di Revel who preferred calculated risk. No such confusion about the final strategy would be allowed once Thaon di Revel was back.

Based on the centralized Italian Anti-Submarine Warfare (ASW) Command created in 1917, the RM had, since 1936, planned a Central Command, which was tested in 1939 and activated in May 1940 and named '*Supermarina*'. Its tasks were to dictate strategy, order general directives, collect information from any source and to initiate orders of operations. Contrary to rumour, the Commander at Sea in fact had total freedom during an engagement; a situation not unlike that of the Admiralty with its admirals or commodores.

In 1940, Admiral Angelo Iachino was appointed the new battlefleet commander. His predecessor Inigo Campioni became the deputy CoS, while Admiral Carlo Bergamini was appointed Inspector of the fitting out of new warships until July 1941, when he went back to sea as commander of the V Divisione formed by the modernized battleships. Iachino asked the new CoS, Admiral Arturo Riccardi, at once for a detailed, written description of his rules of engagement and received a curt reply that the RM tradition was that the commander of the battlefleet was the master, once at sea.

For most of the war against Britain, the RM battlefleet was commanded by Admiral Iachino (9 December 1940–4 April 1943). He was a brilliant destroyer man and a torpedo and optics expert, not primarily a gunnery officer like admirals Campioni and Bergamini. According to a report from British Intelligence written in December 1940, Iachino was:

found to have an attractive personality and he speaks fluent English … While in London as Naval Attaché Iachino adopted a pleasing manner to those officers of similar or superior ranks with whom he came into contact, but was occasionally bad-tempered and, unlike the majority of Italians, he had little sense of humour and resented any form of leg-pulling … he was held in high regard in the Italian Navy and was equally efficient at a desk and at sea; he was, however, not at all popular. He has the reputation of being hard, efficient, stubborn and exceedingly ambitious but without imagination. It is thought that at this time a C. in C. with imagination and human understanding is what the Italians require to pull them together. This is just what this new appointment will not give them.

He was an unlucky man, as the wild goose chase of Force H and the Matapan night battle confirmed in 1941.

His successor, Bergamini, was what the RN Intelligence described as the right man in the right place at the right time. In December 1940, he should have been Campioni's replacement as the new battlefleet commander, as Cavagnari considered Iachino too young and lacking the necessary experience. But politics decided otherwise and Cavagnari was sacked in early December 1940, with many other top-ranking Italian officers – Marshal Badoglio was replaced by his arch-enemy General Ugo Cavallero – when Mussolini tried to put the blame for the Greek fiasco on everyone else's shoulders except his own and those of his son-in-law, Galeazzo Ciano.

The II Squadra was the scouting force of the battleforce. It was commanded first by Admiral Riccardo Paladini and, after he suffered heart failure on 24 July 1940, by Iachino. Abolished on 9 December 1940, the II Squadra was reactivated on 12 January 1942 around the Cavour-class dreadnoughts and was led by Bergamini until 1 January 1943, when he took the place of Iachino, raising his ensign on *Littorio* as commander of the IX Divisione formed by the three modern 35,000t battleships. Iachino was 'promoted' to the command of any joint operations of both the I and II Squadra, a far from probable scenario as the oil available did not allow such operations until the second half of August 1943. On 2 January 1943, the by-now practically autonomous V Divisione (*Duilio* and *Doria*) based at Taranto raised the ensign of Admiral Emilio Brenta, who, on 30 July, was substituted, for reasons of health, by Admiral Alberto Da Zara, by far the most popular and outgoing Italian admiral of World War II.

There were three CoSs of the RM during the war. First was the severe Cavagnari, father of the Littorio class and the battlefleet, and a World War I

Taranto, August 1940. A despatch motorboat bringing sealed orders to the flagship of the battleforce. The RM used hand-delivered messages for its Operations Orders. An exception was the order for air reconnaissance sent by air by a messenger to Rhodes before the Action off Matapan. The aircraft and the Enigma-ciphered message were seized by the British on the night of 26 March 1941, at Crete using a fake radio-beacon. A new message was then broadcast from Rome to Rhodes. ULTRA decrypted the original message within 24 hours, but not the signal sent by radio. (AC)

destroyer man whose personal doctrine about sea control of the Ionian Sea and fighting a long-term tonnage war, mainly by submarines, dominated the conflict. He was replaced, on 11 December 1940, by Riccardi. The new CoS added his personal touch about escort vessels to battleship doctrine (he had been, since 1916, a strenuous supporter of ASW and of the decisive role of the defence of sea lanes) and his faith in mass production. As a result, from 1942, the RM commissioned plenty (by Italian standards, of course) of Ciclone-class destroyer escorts, corvettes, MTBs, motor antisubmarine boats and landing craft.

As the CoS was simultaneously the Secretary of the Navy whose minister, Mussolini, was virtually absent, the leadership of Supermarina was actually in the hands of the Deputy CoS. He was supported by at first four and, from 1941, six admirals, one of them at a time directing, during his watch, the Situation Room. The Deputy CoS were Admiral Odoardo Somigli until 18 December 1940, Admiral Campioni up to 23 July 1941 and Admiral Luigi Sansonetti as late as the days after the Italian armistice. Somigli was rigid and not very popular in the Navy ranks; Campioni was very clear-headed, but suffered bad health; Sansonetti was the powerhouse behind the remaining Italian war at sea.

The communications between Supermarina and the fleet were always efficient, mostly taking place by hand or scrambler telephone for security, and the RM wireless network was, traditionally, the most efficient in the country. In 1940–41, the TPA, a sort of Italian version of the USN TBS ship-to-ship system, was introduced, helping greatly with tactical communications.

INTELLIGENCE AND DECEPTION
SIGINT

The RM codebreaking organization Ufficio B (Beta from the Italian phonetic alphabet) turned from an amateur outfit into a tiny, but operational one in 1931, when the Director of the *Reparto Informazioni dello Stato Maggiore della Marina* (from June 1941 onwards known as the *Servizio Informazioni Segrete* or SIS), Rear-Admiral Alberto Lais, decided to create a professional cryptological section. Two years later, the new Secretary of the Navy (and, in the following year, CoS) Cavagnari, put the organization on a war footing, having foreseen that Mussolini's political strategy would inevitably lead to a crisis with Britain within a few years. The first target of Ufficio B, whose rooms were on the top floor of the Naval Ministry, just a flight of stairs up from Cavagnari's office, was the main French naval cipher, the TMB. It was considered impregnable, but it was cracked within a few weeks. The new versions adopted by Paris the following year, TBM 2 and 3, were quickly broken, and until June 1940 the cipher granted high dividends to the RM.

The next goal was, of course, the British. In November 1934, the Royal Navy's Administrative Naval Code was broken. Twenty-four hours were originally needed to reconstruct the keys, but from 1935 this delay was reduced to a few hours.

The much more complex and more important Naval Cipher proved, however, a harder nut to crack. In 1938, Lieutenant Commander Francesco Camicia, commander of the sloop *Lepanto* stationed in China, was able to 'rent' and photograph over the course of several hours, the first of the two books of the Naval Cipher from an NCO of a British destroyer in Shanghai. The sailor who passed the book to the Italians had been persuaded he was not doing anything really dangerous as, without the second book (*Superencipherment*) with random or incoherent keystreams, the cipher was just a useless dictionary. An initial solution was found after some spy-ship missions in the Mediterranean and in the Atlantic identified pairs and triples of messages superenciphered with the same keystream (the so-called 'depth') which allowed the reconstruction of the relevant superencipher tables. There were gaps, of course, but that cipher remained in use until 20 August 1940. It was necessary to periodically reconstruct the new superciphers introduced every month by cryptologic systems, but it was a task the mathematical methods that Ufficio B created could handle usually in less than a week. The cryptology section was increased, between 1938 and 1939, with the appointment of a dozen new codebreakers, including the magician of tactical signals, Lieutenant Eliso Porta, nicknamed '*Il principe azzurro*' (Prince Charming) for his successes with foreign tactical codes classified by female names, 'Boadicea' and 'Rowena' for the British.

The secret battle fought by the RM codebreakers went on until the Armistice and beyond, as the Italians wanted to be sure the Allies were as good as their word. Although a comparison between signals and the different sets of data is always difficult (as routine radio interceptions made in lower-grade codes are included), between 10 June 1940 and 1 September 1943, RM codebreakers intercepted and decrypted 36,262 British, 209 French pre-armistice, 4,002 French post-armistice, 989 Yugoslavian, and several hundred American, Greek, Free French, Russian and Turkish signals. The decryption times varied from less than 15 minutes for the RAF reconnaissance signals (reduced to under two minutes from January 1942, when the first IBM machines modified in Italy became operative for decrypting purposes) to hours or days in the worst cases.

On 14 July 1940, an intercepted RN message revealed that the British had been able to decrypt a signal broadcast using one of the two new, main RM ciphers introduced on 2 July 1940, the SM 19S, seized three days before on the submarine *Uebi Scebeli*. An emergency order was issued to the effect that, for superenciphering, the initials of the captain of any vessel were to be used pending delivery of a new (currently reserve) cipher to all ships before the end of that month. As Professor Hinsley acknowledged in his famous *British Intelligence in the Second World War*: 'the cyphers used by [the Italian] fleet for most of its important communications were never read again after July 1940 except for a few brief intervals as a result of captures after the middle of 1941'. These few leaks, all concerning administrative codes, were always promptly discovered by the RM codebreakers and used to their advantage, such as during the great British *Crusader* offensive, when the RM, having discovered the Benghazi naval coastal command cipher had been photographed by British Intelligence

DAWN SURPISE: THE BATTLE OF PANTELLERIA, 15 JUNE 1942

On 15 June 1942, the Italian VII Divisione made a completely surprise attack against the Harpoon convoy and its escort force. The assessment of the situation in the Mediterranean the previous day by the Admiralty and Force W from Gibraltar, led by Admiral Alban T. B. Curteis, had incorrectly concluded that the VII Divisione was going to join the main Italian battleforce in the Eastern Mediterranean from Palermo. It instead intercepted the Western convoy for Malta in the mine-infested Strait of Sicily. The scattered British and Allied (one Polish destroyer) force was thus deployed in penny packets, favouring the Italian cruiser squadron which detached the slower destroyers *Ugolino Vivaldi* (28kt; caused by a machinery defect) and *Lanzerotto Malocello* (32kt). They attacked the convoy independently before the smoke curtain, laid by four Hunt destroyers and Fleet minesweepers, made the convoy disappear.

In spite of the much vaunted 'ULTRA' decrypts, British Intelligence about the RM was still pretty poor. The estimated effective strength of the Italian fleet in June 1942 was largely inaccurate: it was not known that the battleship *Vittorio Veneto* had been repaired and had been back at sea since late March 1942, also that three light cruisers and seven destroyers, which were given as sunk, were actually in service, untraced by British intelligence. Information about the RM was categorized as mainly B1 and B2, and even the desperate fuel situation was unknown, in spite of the fact that the waterline of Italian battleships and cruisers showed how little fuel was in their bunkers.

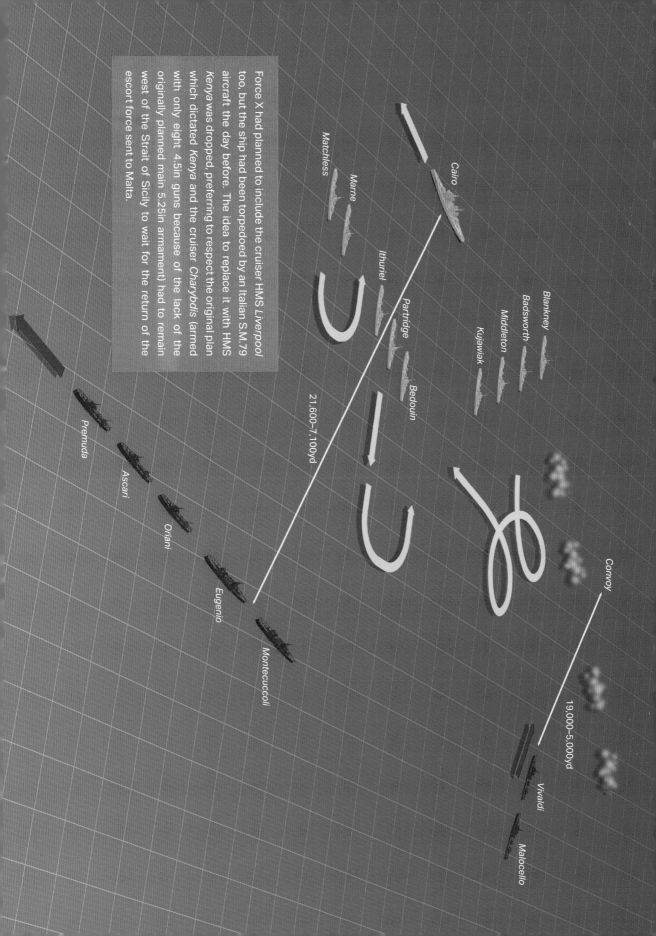

Force X had planned to include the cruiser HMS *Liverpool* too, but the ship had been torpedoed by an Italian S.M.79 aircraft the day before. The idea to replace it with HMS *Kenya* was dropped, preferring to respect the original plan which dictated *Kenya* and the cruiser *Charybdis* (armed with only eight 4.5in guns because of the lack of the originally planned main 5.25in armament) had to remain west of the Strait of Sicily to wait for the return of the escort force sent to Malta.

Matchless

Cairo

Marne

Ithuriel

Partridge

Bedouin

21,600–7,100yd

Blankney

Badsworth

Middleton

Kujawiak

Convoy

Premuda

Ascari

Oriani

Eugenio

Montecuccoli

19,000–5,000yd

Vivaldi

Malocello

The Italian modified Hagelin C-38m mechanical cypering machine. Unlike the Regia Aeronautica low-grade C-35, this medium-grade system was used for administrative signals only and never from ships to ships or land commands. (AC)

two months before, broadcast false messages to deceive Eighth Army HQ that no Axis counter-offensive was planned for months, before it was actually unleashed on 21 January 1942.

The wartime British decryption organization, the Government Code and Cipher School (GC&CS), whose output is commonly known as 'ULTRA', boasted a total of 42,163 decrypted messages (of every origin and nationality) relating to Italian naval affairs in 1941–43, labelled ZTPI and now in The National Archives. Their origin is mainly from mechanical and electromechanical machines (the latter German only) while 3,699 are hand ciphers. These messages were intercepted between 1 April 1940 and 9 September 1943, but around 50 per cent were decoded in 1944–45 for historical and statistical purposes. The times of codebreaking varied between real time (once the machine cipher keys had been broken) to several days for the messages composed using the classic cipher books.

The main Italian leak was the Hagelin C-35 machine, operated from October 1940 by the RA and broken by the British in July 1941. The RM had refused it in 1935 as it considered the Swedish cipher machine unsafe, but the RA preferred the C-35 for everyday communications because of its speed and ease of use. This continued despite the regular protests by the RM, which, from November 1941, used another, more advanced Hagelin machine, the C-38m, but only for administrative traffic, like the daily press review. The C-38m (which was broken by ULTRA in January 1942) was not used by individual warships nor by the commands at sea, which could only receive and read signals sent to them (generally circular letters) encrypted with the system, but not broadcast by the cipher.

The percolation of information from the C-35 ended in January 1943, when the RM reactivated and relaid, in the direction of Italy, two cables between Tunis and Malta which the Italian cable layer *Giasone* had cut on 14 June 1940. This meant that communications between Tunisia–Sicily and the Italian peninsula could no longer be intercepted over the airwaves. From that point until the Italian Armistice, the importance of ULTRA intercepts of Italian signals declined dramatically. They had been, however, always a lower priority compared to the German Enigma signals, and it often took 96 hours or even more for Bletchley Park to send Italian decrypts to the Intelligence Centre of Heliopolis, in Egypt.

HUMINT

Agents played a minor role on both sides during the naval war in the Mediterranean. In May 1940, the British were able to seize the Italian spy network in the UK (actually a group of White Russians infiltrated by the NKVD, the People's Commissariat for Internal Affairs, who were also active in the US Embassy in London, and were loaned from Soviet intelligence to Rome in 1935). Two years later, the RM had a new agent in Britain, the Portuguese embassy clerk Rogério de Magalhães Peixoto de Menezes, who on 24 September 1942 sent, via Ireland, some very detailed information about the future Anglo-American landings in French North Africa. Once other details were added, this source allowed *Comando Supremo* (the Italian General Staff) to be ready, between late October and the landing on 8 November, to occupy Tunisia from Italy and Libya, in spite of Germany's disbelief in such an Allied invasion.

Unfortunately, in 1943, Rogério also decided to work for the SS intelligence agency *Reichssicherheitshauptamt* (RSHA) and was sold out to British counterespionage within two weeks. Condemned to be hanged, he was saved by the direct intervention of the Italian royal household and liberated in 1949 as a courtesy to Rome after the signature of the NATO treaty of alliance.

All 20 agents sent by the Special Operations Executive (SOE) to Italy in 1941–43 were either captured, unknowingly used by Italian counterintelligence, or at worst, forcibly turned as double agents. False information about the imminent commissioning of the repaired battleship *Cavour,* which arrived on Admiral Pound's desk in December 1941 and was accepted until the Italian Armistice, originated from deceptions such as this.

LOGISTICS AND FACILITIES

The RM's stocks of spare parts and related domestic production was never in short supply during World War II except between 1940 and 1941, for high-tensile steel for hulls and copper and mica for electrical equipment. In 1943, depots and wrecks in the Toulon dockyard were ransacked for these strategic materials. The manufacturing of anti-aircraft munitions was always a hand-to-mouth affair, which compelled Italian air defences to avoid barrage fire, day or night, and only to aim to shoot when the target was sighted or illuminated by searchlights.

No warships bigger than a destroyer were constructed during wartime. This was not unexpected: since 1931, assessments had been made on the consequences of a conflict with Britain, and wartime construction of both warships and merchant vessels accorded with these. Italy correctly forecast the amount of raw materials and workforce which would be realistically available.

The dispersed network of Italian yards and arsenals allowed a certain degree of security against air raids. Before the Armistice, only the OTO enterprise of Livorno was seriously damaged, on 28 May 1943, by USAAF bombers.

The main naval bases were La Spezia and Taranto. Naples and La Maddalena could receive the battlefleet, but had only minor facilities. Messina, Cagliari, Augusta, Venice, Pola and Brindisi could supply and support a cruiser squadron. Tobruk, Leros, Massawa, Tripoli and Trapani were bases for light forces formed by destroyers, torpedo boats, MTBs and submarines.

The British were much worse off without Malta, unavailable from 1940 onwards due to the air threat, and whose main docks would be filled with debris and wrecks until the end of the war. The limited facilities available at Alexandria and Gibraltar forced the RN to avoid risking serious damage which could only be repaired at Durban, Singapore, at home or in the USA. When recaptured in 1943 and 1944 respectively, the ports of Bizerte and Toulon were found in ruins, and the only major yard the Allies could use during the Italian Campaign was the intact Taranto.

The real problem for the RM was oil. In mid-August 1940, Mussolini ordered that oil stocks should last until early 1942, as the original prediction about a three-month war had been wrong. The

Taranto, August 1940. The destroyer *Carducci* and the submarine *Serpente* in a dock for refit and maintenance. The larger Italian yard facilities as opposed to the poorer British ones in the Mediterranean provided key back-up to the Italian Navy during the war. (AC)

original RM reserves of fuel were empty by the end of September 1941. From June 1941, supplies from Romania (mainly by rail) to the RM amounted to a monthly average of 35,000t. After a lone, emergency German aid of 81,000t was shipped between late November 1941 and January 1942, German supplies crashed, and between April 1942 and July 1943 Germany sent, irregularly, a total of a further 333,000t of mostly synthetic fuel oil, with unexpected pauses between shipments as long as three months.

The activity of La Squadra was thus progressively paralysed from summer 1942 until early March 1943, when increased production of Albanian oil arrived in Italy, allowing the RM to fill the empty bunkers of the Littorios in April and of the two Duilios after 20 July for some short-range training and a last do-or-die sortie.

COMBAT AND ANALYSIS

THE FLEET IN COMBAT

On 26 January 1939, the British Admiralty discussed a swift, mainly naval war against Italy with the MN. Paris answered enthusiastically. British opinion was that the RM was a 'sugar cake navy' and, in March 1939, Winston Churchill, then a backbench MP, argued that Italy's exposed geographical position and lack of resources made it a hindrance to its Axis partner.[6]

In April 1939, Italy invaded Albania with an improvised landing; the second round was the invasion of Greece, scheduled for September 1939. Mussolini and General Alberto Pariani, Secretary of War and his main military adviser from 1934, both wrongly believed that the Anglo-French would accept such a fait accompli, while the USSR (which had been an excellent economic partner to Italy since 1920) would want to get its hands on the Bosporus and Dardanelles Straits. Britain and France collaborated, at the same time, planning and supporting a Turkish landing at Rhodes that autumn. However, the Danzig Crisis unleashed by Hitler against Poland in August 1939 prevented any of these plans from going ahead. It was soon clear that any real chance for an Allied victory would pass through Italy.

The Outbreak of War

The Allied naval blockade was considered to be as effective as it had been in 1914–15. The difference was that what the Allies now looked for in Italy was not a potential ally but a good battlefield. In September 1939, Cavagnari asked for the conversion of the liner *Roma* into the slow emergency aircraft carrier planned in 1935. At first the plan seemed to be on the right track and the fighters for the ship, Caproni Vizzola F.5, were chosen, but, in November 1939, the newly appointed CoS of the RA, General Francesco Pricolo, brought everything to a stop.

---

6   Churchill, W.S., *Step by Step*, Thornton Butterworth Ltd, London, 1939.

On 1 March 1940, it was announced that German coal exports to Italy, sent by sea via Dutch ports, would be prohibited. The Allies were aware of the fact that German exports of coal by railway through Austria and Yugoslavia could cover only 50 per cent of Italy's peacetime consumption (one million tons monthly) and that Switzerland had closed its borders to this rail traffic in September 1939.

As soon as the puzzled French Prime Minister Édouard Daladier (a much more prudent man since the Molotov–Ribbentrop Pact was unexpectedly signed on 23 August 1939) was replaced, on 21 March 1940, by the battling Paul Reynaud, the Allied concentration of naval forces in the Mediterranean began. The previous build-up, inaugurated by the return to Toulon in July 1939 of the three Bretagnes, had been halted by force majeure in August 1939 due to the imminent danger of war with Germany. Between April and May 1940, the Mediterranean Fleet (which had left Malta for Alexandria in April 1939), rallied four battleships (*Warspite*, *Malaya*, *Royal Sovereign* and *Ramillies*) and the carrier *Eagle*, while since April 1940, the French had had three Bretagnes and two Dunkerques in the Mediterranean. The so-called 'Mediterranean Stoppage' – the end of Britain's route through the Strait of Sicily – was introduced on 30 April.

On 9 May 1940, *Dunkerque* and *Strasbourg* sailed from Mers-el-Kébir to search, near Sardinia, for the Italian battlefleet (which was formed, at that time, by the reconstructed battleships *Cavour* and *Cesare* only). Their mission was halted the day after, as the Germans had unleashed their invasion of Western Europe. After a series of last-minute diplomatic skirmishes, Italy declared war on 10 June 1940, with less than 30 days of coal stocks. Like the British at Malta, the French limited themselves to using their big naval base at Bizerte for light forces (destroyers and submarines), given the Italian bomber menace, the RM's large minefields and submarines, and their night-time torpedo boats and MAS patrols. On 16 June, the French Admiral François Darlan, commander-in-chief of the MN, declared to the French government that Italian control of the Strait of Sicily meant that Allied navies and

Eastern Mediterranean, 8 July 1940. HMS *Malaya* slightly damaged by a near-miss bomb dropped by a Cant Z 506 flying boat. Splinters temporarily impaired her forward HA guns. This accident was not reported in the British official report. (AC)

air forces could not prevent the arrival within a couple of months of a German corps in Libya. This force would be able to advance to Morocco before Britain, still disarmed after Dunkirk, could send any help to the 'unreinforçable', badly equipped French army stationed between Tunisia and Casablanca. This statement was the last nail in the coffin for a French continuation of the war in Africa, supported by only a minority of the Reynaud cabinet (who resigned later that evening).

On 25 June, the Axis' armistices with France came into effect and Bern immediately opened its railways to coal traffic bound for Italy, which would continue until February 1945. For years, Switzerland also supplied the many extra trains necessary for the task.

The MN battleforce was divided between Mers-el-Kébir and Alexandria, and its fate was respectively in the hands of Vice-Admiral James Somerville's recently formed Force H at Gibraltar, and Vice-Admiral Andrew Browne Cunningham. With the French out of the war, it was an Anglo-Italian conflict, as the now-Prime Minister Churchill broadcast on 18 June: 'There is a general curiosity in the British Fleet to find out whether the Italians are up to the level they were at in the last war or whether they have fallen off at all'.

The first move by Cunningham, commander-in-chief of the Mediterranean Fleet, was to send a wireless message to the Admiralty on 4 July with his battle order and plan for a demonstration off the Eastern Sicilian coast. He could have used the cables between Egypt, Malta, Gibraltar and Britain as the last underwater telegraphic link between the Rock and the Grand Harbour would only be severed by the Italians the following month, but he was in a hurry after the many signals from Churchill urging him to neutralize the French squadron in Alexandria and had no time for the many relays it demanded. His signal was decrypted by the RM codebreakers on the night of 4/5 July and Supermarina decided to give battle to the Italian battlefleet[7] which had just escorted a decisive convoy to Benghazi, ferrying the only 72 medium tanks (M11/39 type) existing in Italy there.

The Action off Calabria (*Battaglia di Punta Stilo*)

From early morning onwards on 9 July, despite some gaps, British air reconnaissance was able to follow the Italian battleforce, now formed by I Squadra with battleships *Cesare*, Campioni's flagship, and *Cavour*, plus five heavy cruisers; also the scouting force II Squadra, led by Admiral Riccardo Paladini in his flagship *Pola*, and eight light cruisers, escorted by 29 destroyers, off the coast of Calabria. Italian aircraft saw and signalled the presence of the Mediterranean Fleet for the first time at 1330hrs: battleships *Warspite* (Cunningham's flagship), *Royal Sovereign* and *Malaya*, with carrier *Eagle*; the scouting force was Admiral Tovey's 7th Cruiser Squadron, with flagship *Orion*

---

7 Like most of the apparently indecisive naval actions made by the RM, the wartime British and Italian narratives of events differ. Here the RM version is described – much less known outside Italy.

and a further four light cruisers and 17 destroyers. Supermarina was aware of the enemy's overwhelming advantage in firepower and armour (8in guns were unable at any range to pierce the battleships' protection), but placed their confidence in the Cavours' speed advantage over the British battleships, which would allow them to stay out of range. Italian naval intelligence about RN fire-direction had been updated until the mid-1930s but was not aware of later progress, including the increasingly automatic Admiralty-Fire-Control-Table Mark VII fitted in *Warspite* in 1937. It therefore reported that the British were unable to match the long range of the Cavours' 12.6in while the AP shells of the Italian guns (bored-out old 12in weapons) were considered as very effective. It was believed too that RN fire-control was not as effective as the Italians'. As the main action began, it was soon discovered that *Warspite*, modernized in 1934–37, had increased her 15in guns' elevation to 30 degrees and that her fire-control was excellent even though other RN cruisers were confirmed to be out of line (most of them were equipped with less expensive Fire-Control-Tables). What the RM did not know was that the middle deck (now with an overall 5in protection over the magazines) of Cunningham's flagship could not be pierced at any range by the reconstructed Italian battleships.

According to the British Official Report on the Action off Calabria, dated 29 January 1941, the first phase of the battle, involving scouting forces, was an engagement between four heavy cruisers of the Zara class and four RN light cruisers (HMS *Gloucester*, hit by a bomb the day before by a surprise attack from out of nowhere, was at that time escorting *Eagle* as her fighting efficiency had been impaired). The Italian force was only composed of the light cruisers *Abruzzi* (Admiral Antonio Legnani) and *Garibaldi*, forming VIII Divisione with four destroyers – the original report by HMS *Neptune* confirms both their number and the fact they were correctly identified. The steady fire of the semi-automatic 6in of the Garibaldis straddled the 7th Cruiser Squadron almost at once, whose course had soon to be altered away to avoid getting too heavily engaged. *Neptune* was slightly damaged amidships by splinters which were identified, given the excellent fragmentation of the Italian navy shells, as being from 12in projectiles. According to the RN rules of engagement, Cunningham was in the vanguard position relative to his other battleships, to act as a sort of battlecruiser. He was thus able to give his support some minutes later, firing at VIII Divisione. In his memoirs Cunningham wrote he steamed at flank speed (23kt) to support his cruisers, but the Navigational Record of *Warspite* states he slowed from 20 to 17kt so as not to stray too far from his slower two battleships astern, it being necessary to concentrate his forces at the crucial moment.

Warspite began ineffective fire against the Garibaldis. Legnani in *Abruzzi* did not alter his course, in order to perform his scouting mission to the best of his ability. Then, not having been sighted by the British, the light cruisers *Alberto di Giussano* and *Alberico da Barbiano*, joined the action and opened fire against *Warspite*. At 1527hrs, *Di Giussano* (the flagship of Rear-Admiral Da Zara) observed a direct hit on the forebridge of the British battleship which immediately made a round 360-degree turn.

However, the British official report, published in 1948 (itself a digest of the Battle Summary made in 1942 for RN internal use) offered an alternative explanation: that the explosion had not been a shell hit from the RM ships, but one of *Warspite*'s Swordfish floatplanes on the catapult that was damaged by X turret's muzzle blast and subsequently jettisoned. The official version is not backed by the primary evidence.[8]

Legnani and, some minutes later, the two small Condottieris (IV Divisione) emerged unscathed and turned away at 1530hrs after accomplishing their scouting task which gave Campioni and Paladini the chance to establish the best course and position of tactical advantage, before joining the action.

When the main action between the battleships began, at 1553hrs, *Warspite* was still too far from *Royal Sovereign* and *Malaya*, but Campioni, deceived by the visual perspective, believed the enemy force had reunited.

---

8   The testimony of *Warspite*'s Swordfish pilot (recorded by Iain Ballantyne in his book *Warspite*) stated that that day the battleship only had one Swordfish which was catapulted at 1548hrs, as the Italians also observed. The other Swordfish had been shot down near Tobruk, on 21 June, by two FIAT CR.32 fighters and its aircrew, recovered at sea the next day, would become inmates of the Italian Navy camp of Poveglia, near Venice. To compensate for that loss, the British decided to convert one of *Eagle*'s 18 Swordfish to a floatplane, but the British historian Ray Sturtivant documented in *The Swordfish Story* that conversion was completed at Dekheila only at the end of July. An accident to a Swordfish floatplane put out of action by a blast *did* happen on 9 July, but it was on *Malaya*, at 1608hrs, and only because a defect had jammed the ship's double-ended catapult. Further 6in damage recorded by *Warspite* abreast No.2-4in mounting caused minor structural damage, mainly splinter effect, and was ascribed to a near-miss bomb dropped on 8 July, but the Bombing Summary for that day says: 'nearest bomb 70yds from *Warspite*; no damage or casualties'.

9 JULY 1940, 1557hrs: THE ACTION OFF CALABRIA (*BATTAGLIA DI PUNTA STILO*)   (overleaf)

Between June 1940 and May 1943, the defence of the Sicilian Strait and the Ionian Sea was an Italian prerogative. In the illustration, an 8in shell directly hits *Warspite*'s main topmast. The HE projectile fired at *Warspite* is from the heavy cruiser *Trento*. Italian crews then observed a hard turn of the ship, manoeuvering to evade and closing her X and Y arcs. Until June 1943, Italian naval strategy was based on the experience of this battle: the Cavours had been able to fight modernized British battleships; Admiral Fioravanzo's theory that initial long-range attack was decisive in breaking the psycological balance was proved accurate; and the subsequent medium-range phase, during which the rate of fire could increase, might not materialize depending on the superiority of the opposing forces. These experiences equated to the RN doctrine of initial rapid, accurate fire in order to establish early fire-dominance in a battle. For the RM, almost everything depended on the psychology of the enemy, and the RM was convinced they had gained the upper hand during this action.

In 1957, Captain Roskill wrote in his book *HMS Warspite* that there were so many unpublished Admiralty documents about *Warspite* that the critical reader could not have access to them: 'I have therefore felt it preferable to omit all references to unpublished sources, even though I realise the dangers and disadvantages of doing so'.

Action off Calabria, 9 July 1940. The battleship *Cesare*, seen from her sistership *Cavour*, has just fired her first half salvo (five rounds) against HMS *Malaya*. (AC)

He changed the previous order of concentrating his two battleships' fire against *Warspite*, instead ordering each to concentrate on the two nearest battleships out of the three. Although Campioni was a very brilliant officer and gunnery expert, who in 1936 had introduced the modern RM fire-control doctrine (almost identical to the RN's), he was becoming elderly and unfit. His staff considered his visual interpretation of the situation wrong, but the very rigid rules of the RM did not encourage subordinates to contradict him. Only his CoS, Bergamini, would have had the chance to correct the commander-in-chief of the *Squadre riunite* (the joint I and II Squadra) but, as the father of the new 15in gun system, he had been sent to Taranto in May to fix the many teething troubles of the brand new Littorios, not yet in service, and his role had been filled by Admiral Bruto Brivonesi, commander of V Divisione (the two Cavours) and unfortunately perhaps the most rigid officer in the whole navy.

Cesare thus began to fire at *Malaya*, and *Cavour* against *Royal Sovereign* at the extreme range of 31,000yds. In spite of such an astronomical distance, *Cavour*'s opening salvo was fairly accurate and straddled its target before the British battleship was covered by changing its place in line with the faster *Malaya*. *Royal Sovereign* suffered some minor underwater damage, such as rivets having popped and sea water getting into the fresh water tanks and her speed dropped from 18 to 16.5kt. She was temporarily repaired at Durban, South Africa, two months later and then at Gibraltar. These accidents were later imputed to bombs but the Bombing Summaries do not support this version as the nearest bomb (which missed her) during the whole six-day operation was on 10 July, 100yds from her starboard side.

Only *Warspite* replied, as the other two battleships were out of range: turrets A and B fired on *Cesare* and X and Y on *Cavour*. One gun from each turret fired in each salvo, but her rate of fire was (according to British tradition since Crécy) rapid over accurate, in order to establish early fire-dominance. The Italian modernized battleships fired only at half the rate of fire of the enemy's; their guns had to be loaded at +12 degrees with a maximum elevating speed of 6 degrees/sec (*Warspite* +5 degrees and *Malaya* +20 degrees, both 5 degree/sec). Each ship fired five or six projectiles in each salvo.

Admiral Carlo Cattaneo (III Divisione), whose flagship *Trento* was the last of the line of II Squadra after it had turned 180 degrees in unison, saw some minutes after that Cunningham's flagship was not engaged by any Italian ships; he opened fire on *Warspite* on his own initiative for as long as the range of his 8in guns allowed him to, while heading north with the other Italian heavy cruisers to engage the 7th Cruiser Squadron. *Trento*'s First Gunnery Officer saw the range passing from salvos to broadsides. At 1557hrs, an 8in HE direct hit by *Trento* was seen on the battleship aft, both by the Italian ships and the Ro.43 floatplanes catapulted by the RM cruisers. It was followed by some blue smoke.

The British official report stated later the Italian shooting during the action was not good and that most of the salvos fell within 1,000yds from *Warspite* except for one closely bunched salvo which fell about two cables from Cunningham's flagship. But the original reports written in July 1940 tell a different story, from 'extremely accurate' Italian shooting against *Warspite* to: '1554 … Splashes seen falling round *Warspite*.'[9] The damage was along the flying deck on the starboard side. The M.3 pom-pom was put out of service and its ready-to-use magazine was ignited by splinters while the .50in machine gun crews on X turret were blown over. Other superficial damage from splinters were: the crane topping lift wire cut, a hole in the aft end of the funnel and another in the crow's nest; some Carley floats and boats were also pierced.[10]

After the hit observed on *Warspite*, the Italians recorded that the battleship had swung out of line to port, heading south-west along a new, and this time diverging, route compared to the Italian one, while *Trento* was, by now, too far to fire against that target.

Action off Calabria, 9 July 1940, 1603hrs. A near-miss 12.6 shell fired by turret Y of *Cesare* which fell over, seen from HMS *Malaya* a few seconds after the explosion. It detonated abreast the starboard quarter of the unprotected bow of HMS *Warspite*. The 200ft-tall water columns behind the ship are from the previous half salvo (two rounds) fired by turrets X and Y about 15 seconds before. *Warspite*'s speed is 17kt. (AC)

---

9 HMS *Hasty* Proceeding.

10 According to a later version dated 1942 *Warspite* also received a near-miss bomb on 12 July damaging that part of the ship, but the Bombing Summary did not record the damage.

The signals among the British warships included a sharp reprimand to *Malaya*, made during the same minute of that swing to port, to follow the flagship's movements. However, the issue with *Malaya* was that at 1600hrs the wheel in the Upper Conning Tower had jammed to coincide with a straddled salvo by *Cesare*, and orders to the Control Engine Room steering had to be passed from the Compass Platform by voicepipe.

Malaya was docked for five days between 5 and 10 August 1940 for permanent repairs as soon as the new moon granted a certain security against enemy air raids. *Warspite* was taken in hand for permanent repairs during the following two days. Repairs to *Cesare* were finished on 31 July.

One shell (labelled by Cunningham as 'lucky') of the last salvo fired by *Warspite*, before her alteration of course affected firing, hit *Cesare*'s aft funnel at 1559hrs, exploding inside it. The cap was projected outside the funnel and was stopped by the internal face of the main armoured belt, but during its run it set fire to 4.7in charges stored in a lower-deck unprotected storeroom. This was against regulations and a bad way to increase the secondary armament's rate of fire. The smoke caused the shutdown, for some minutes, of four boilers. The course remained steady and *Cesare* passed to shoot against *Warspite*, while *Cavour* was still firing at *Royal Sovereign*.

At 1603hrs, the First Gunnery Officer of *Cesare* observed what was considered as a near-miss, noting *Warspite* was suddenly bow-heavy and listing at a considerable angle to starboard. A second later, one 12.6in direct hit was observed (confirmed by the photo on page 46). The Ro.43 of the cruiser *Eugenio* reported what was called '*una zampata*' (a blow with a paw) on the British flagship. *Warspite* recorded and assigned credit for some further minor damages by splinters, this time in the starboard after the end of the screen around the Admiral's bridge; the Flag Deck, Signal Deck, HA rangefinder and searchlight platform, from a bomb never claimed by the Italian Air Force. Cunningham's flagship stopped shooting for some minutes and *Malaya*, while

ACTION OFF CALABRIA: THE MAIN PHASE, PART II

After firing and inflicting mutual damage, the battleships *Cesare* and *Warspite* were divided by a smokescreen laid by the Italian destroyers. *Warspite* had counterbalanced a list to starboard down by the stern and was able to fire again with her main armament, this time against the destroyers of the XII Squadriglia through a gap in the smoke curtain. She too was sighted, however, across a similar gap, by the cruiser *Zara* which shot 30 8in HE rounds. Two near-misses damaged the battleship's hull and waterplane area, and she developed an immediate list to port. *Warspite* turned away, not shooting a single round, and *Malaya* replied, firing five salvos, all short, until both sides were covered, once more, by the smoke curtain. Admiral Cunningham, according to a commander of his staff, was very irritated and, on the morning of 13 July, back at Alexandria, wrote to the First Lord, Admiral Pound, about the 'disappointing action' and the fact that: 'The shooting of the enemy cruisers and battleships was generally reported as being of fairly high standard', adding that 'The damaged ship is a nightmare especially one 900 miles from her base'. He also added that the Italian ships with their 'excess of at least five knots' outmanoeuvred the Mediterranean Fleet.

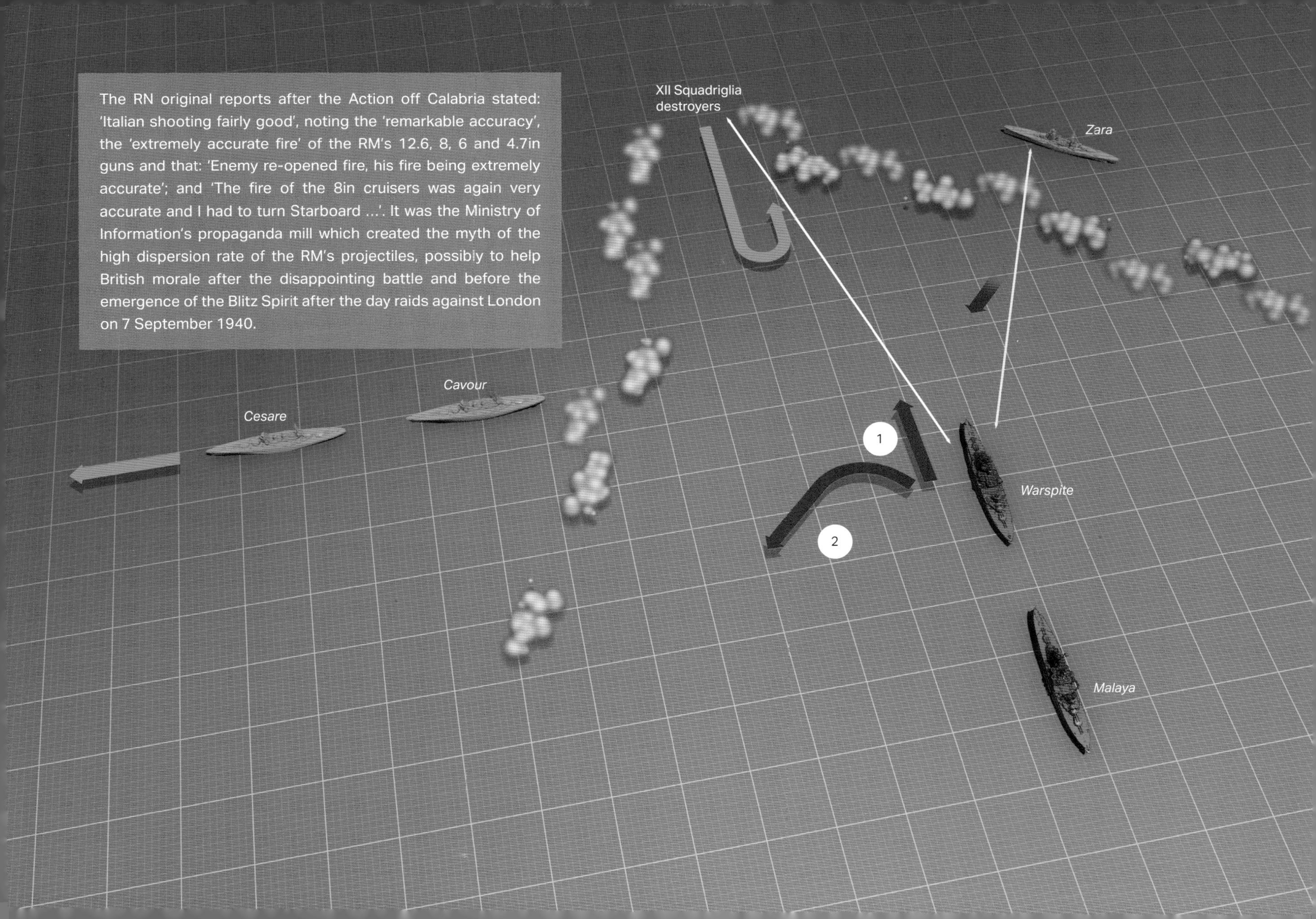

The RN original reports after the Action off Calabria stated: 'Italian shooting fairly good', noting the 'remarkable accuracy', the 'extremely accurate fire' of the RM's 12:6, 8, 6 and 4.7in guns and that: 'Enemy re-opened fire, his fire being extremely accurate'; and 'The fire of the 8in cruisers was again very accurate and I had to turn Starboard ...'. It was the Ministry of Information's propaganda mill which created the myth of the high dispersion rate of the RM's projectiles, possibly to help British morale after the disappointing battle and before the emergence of the Blitz Spirit after the day raids against London on 7 September 1940.

Cesare

Cavour

XII Squadriglia
destroyers

2

1

Warspite

Zara

Malaya

Warspite at Alexandria, August 1940, in the foreground, after repairs. The plating of the stem post peppered by a 12.6in near-miss has been substituted with new red plates yet to be finally painted. Near the waterline, ahead of turret A, can be seen the effects of an oblique (about 28°) direct hit observed by *Cesare* at 1603hrs that penetrated the armour deck, bursting behind the plates after hitting the vessel. The explosion's blast and fire were mild, and material damage was slight. The hard cap made a hole in the upper 6in belt while some fragments pierced the ship's side above. (AWM 18539972)

still out of range, fired for the first time. The distant and too-slow *Royal Sovereign* remained silent. Meanwhile, by 1605hrs the speed of *Cesare* was dropping from 25 to 18kt. Three minutes later, the Italian battleships turned north-west under the protection of a smokescreen laid, from 1606hrs, by two attending destroyers. II Squadra followed, fighting the 7th Cruiser Squadron until 1620hrs.

At 1610hrs, the heavy cruiser *Zara* sighted, through a gap in the smoke, *Warspite* (which, according to the Italian narrative, had rapidly righted herself) and began to fire HE broadsides against her. The British flagship did not answer, but hauled hard to port and *Malaya* had to intervene, again without success. *Zara* appreciated having scored two near-misses, observing that *Warspite*'s trim was down by the head and the ship was rapidly heeling to port, not lurching, but listing heavily, taking on water forward. This incident too is supported by photographic evidence. A couple of minutes later, everything disappeared in the smoke. The Italian floatplane *Eugenio* independently confirmed all these statements, as did a photograph taken by the Navy observer of a S.81 bomber at 1643hrs.

Warspite could have counterflooded easily and within a few minutes to minimize the list caused by the 12.6in near-miss to her stempost that the Italians had noted, transferring some hundred tons of fuel oil and water, however, RN doctrine was not to add sea water for counterflooding. This was because of the cautionary tale of the battleship *Marlborough* which was torpedoed at Jutland with initially relatively little damage and only 800t of salt water inside, but flooding worsened during the following day and threatened to sink her.

With Malta too dangerous for a stay of longer than one night, *Warspite* would take at least two days to arrive at Alexandria – a harbour whose narrow 'Great Pass' was so shallow that a battleship with a 10-degree list would be unable to enter.

On 12 July, an Italian aircraft photographed what was identified as a battleship proceeding independently to Alexandria (*Warspite* that day) with

a list of 7 degrees to port; a trim that would have been quite uncomfortable for the crew.

On the morning of the 13 July, *Warspite* entered Alexandria. Cunningham wrote in his memoirs that people were perturbed to notice that the battleship was heeling over. He explained the battleship had been purposely listed to see if the bulges had been damaged by near-misses, a possibility ruled out by the Bombing Summaries, also because the trim of any ship is constantly monitored and controlled by the inclinometer on the navigating bridge, by the pitch and roll equipment in the engine room, and by the draft marks painted on the sides of any vessel. Temporary patch-up repairs only (according to Italian HUMINT intelligence reports) helped to gain time to weld the torn plating of the hull and the weakened bulges later in the floating dock.

It is worth noting that in August 1940, on the basis of the recent action, the Vice-Chief of Naval Staff, Rear-Admiral T.S.V. Phillips, decided to reduce the thickness of armour abreast the machinery and on the barbettes from 15in to 14in on the planned, future battleships of the Lion class, and to add a 1½in splinter belt on the waterline fore and aft of the citadel, 1in transverse splinter bulkheads between the lower and middle decks, and additional splinter plating to the bridges. The purpose was to prevent the loss of waterplane area at the ends of the ships caused by splinters from shells or bombs exploding outboard, peppering the waterline, and to reduce the area of splinter damage onboard. A similar description of damages was observed by the Italians on 9 July. A confirmation, after the only 19,000–7,000yds Action of the River Plate, that near-misses were possible, and more frequent than envisaged, during the battleships' long-range encounters, and that protection against big guns' heavy splinters had thus to be extended.

During the last phase of this confused action, the Mediterranean Fleet steamed north, from 1620hrs until 1708hrs, according to the Official Report, trying to engage the enemy battlefleet again. The Italians, who were steaming west until 1645hrs, when *Cesare* recovered her original speed, said the British course was south-west towards Malta. The four destroyers of the Italian 12ª

Alexandria, July 1940. Further evident signs of the gunfire damage sustained by *Warspite*. The hole (a 6in HE direct hit by the cruiser *Di Giussano*) in the charthouse and the damage to the waterline under turret X caused by two 8in HE near-misses fired by the cruiser *Zara* at 1613hrs. (AWM 18539972)

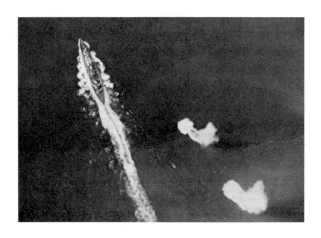

9 July 1940, 1643hrs. HMS *Warspite* seen by a S. 81 bomber. The battleship is stern-heavy and has taken a port list confirmed by the two different wakes. Eddies starboard are connected to the holes in the stem post and the gash caused by the 12.6in cone as seen above. Her pumps are able to control the flooding by clever damage-control procedures. (AC)

Squadriglia engaged for more than half an hour what they regarded as the Mediterranean Fleet sailing south, dodging inside and outside their smokescreen, firing spasmodically and launching torpedoes before coming back under the cover of their curtain, being counterattacked and targeted by the British. The Proceeding of the destroyer *Hereward* confirms the course south of the RN squadron at 1640hrs. At 1700hrs, the Italian level bombers – which had to attack before gunnery action – appeared, dropping their bombs, by that time too far away from each other to engage again. The carrier *Eagle*, the destroyer *Hero* and the cruisers *Gorizia* and *Luigi Cadorna* had some small splinter damage to their decks and some casualties.

Intelligence was supplied to Italy by a Hungarian military attaché in Egypt who had seen (using his binoculars) the warships (two battleships, one carrier, three cruisers and five destroyers) damaged at Alexandria. The information was confirmed, on 21 July, by one member of the crew of a Swordfish floatplane lent by *Malaya* to *Warspite* two days before, who had ditched after an engine failure near Tobruk before being rescued by the Italians. Mussolini himself (who supervised the Italian war bulletins) announced on 22 July the names of the RN warships which had suffered major damage during the recent action (*Warspite* and *Gloucester*, actually hit by a bomb on 8 July and some fragments the next day), information which until then had not been published anywhere. In London, the Ministry of Information denied this at once, but a few days later the obituary, published by the British press, of the captain of *Gloucester* and of 33 men of his warship, turned out to be a catalyst which prompted the press to be more accurate in future reporting.

Consequences of the Battle

Italian records weren't impartial, and with records varying so much, some details of the battle cannot be satisfactorily established. What matters, however, are the following conclusions from the day of action.

To Cunningham, the battle confirmed what the Admiralty had tested at home and then observed in Spain between 1935 and 1939: that high-level bombers had very little chance of hitting a moving battleship, only ships moored in a harbour; also that the submarine menace could only be combated by the recently introduced ASDIC (sonar).[11] Thus, only the

---

11 The latter was just what was missing during the confrontations with Italy between summer 1935 and summer 1937, when the possible loss of a battleship to a submarine or mine would have altered the delicate balance of power in the Far East to a critical extent. Until winter 1938/39, Britain considered a possible reconstruction of the old battleship *Iron Duke* to make up for the loss of a capital ship to torpedoes or mines in the Mediterranean.

Italian battleforce was able to seriously interfere with the RN operations in the Ionian Sea because Italian long-range gunnery and the 12.6in AP shells were effective.

The Italian admirals considered the Action off Calabria (they called it: *Battaglia di Punta Stilo*) a tactical and strategic success. Campioni and Paladini ended the battle with a Parthian shot, complimenting each other by wireless that afternoon. Their signals were intercepted. There is no trace, however, in the 'Action off Calabria 9th July 1940 – List of Enemy Signals Intercepted' record of the alleged submarine trap which would have induced Cunningham (like Lord Jellicoe in 1916) not to pursue the battle. After having asked – and obtained – plenty of reinforcements (battleships, armoured carriers, heavy cruisers, etc.) to shore-up the Mediterranean Fleet, the commander-in-chief wrote about what was later called, because of the battle's unsatisfactory result, the 'myth of moral ascendancy'.

From a tactical point of view, Cunningham described Calabria as a 'very disappointing' action. The rest of the strategic story is pretty clear. For men born in the 19th century, formed by reading Mahan on the 'great naval decisive battle', the Action off Calabria was the missed opportunity of the conflict. It could be compared to the Battle of Ouessant fought between the French and the British on 27 July 1778, an apparently indecisive action which opened the Atlantic sea routes from continental Europe to North America during the United States War of Independence.

There was, however, a fundamental difference. In 1778, Rochambeau and Lafayette had embarked a sufficient number of expeditionary corps, adequately trained and equipped to take on the British Army in North America, while in 1940, the 72 M11/39 tanks of the Regio Esercito (that the naval convoy had safely landed at Benghazi) had to face, between 8 July and late September 1940, no fewer than 85 British A9 and A10 medium tanks which were waiting for them, with better-trained crews, south of Marsa Matruh. And 23 of the 72 Italian tanks were out of order for months after the advance to Sidi Barrani in September 1940. At that time, Suez was already able to receive three times the number of merchant vessels entering Libyan harbours every month. It is evident that Fioravanzo's theory that the army was the decisive force, and the navy's role was just to open the gates of naval traffic and control local seas, was flawed. More sensible was Cavagnari's idea to win the war at sea, and by sea only, bleeding white British tonnage. Italy could survive with sufficient supplies from Europe delivered mainly by railways; the huge British Empire needed, instead, large amounts of maritime traffic whose total tonnage was, since June 1940, declining every month.

The Action off Calabria was the biggest battle at sea fought in Europe, Africa and America during World War II. A further six major daytime actions followed and dozens of other ones, most of them at night (where the RN enjoyed a clear advantage after developing new strategies and radar sets) until the Italian armistice was announced on 8 September 1943.

The Convoy War

After this not-so-decisive 'great naval battle', the Mediterranean naval war turned into a daily guerrilla war fought by expendable means (aircraft, submarines, mines, sometimes light forces) against Axis communications with North Africa and the Balkans. According to reports, 83.49 per cent of the materials and 91.99 per cent of the personnel sent by sea to Libya, Egypt and Tunisia arrived safely, not to mention the respective 99.6 and 99.9 per cent which arrived safe and well in the Balkans.

The average amount of materials delivered to North African ports on a monthly basis was, during the campaign, 65,000t, i.e. the maximum load the poorly equipped harbours could handle and transfer with the insufficient number of trucks available (except during the few periods of standstill along the front, when more lorries were available). There was only one month of crisis, November 1941, when only 37.67 per cent of the supplies sent arrived in Libya, but this didn't affect things as much as it could have, firstly, because Axis stocks in North Africa were always sufficient for one to two months and secondly, the build-up for the planned German and Italian offensive against Tobruk was completed by September 1941 (it was deferred only by the two months' delay needed to complete the *Strada dell'Asse* (Axis Road) around the besieged Tobruk fortress beyond the range of the British heavy artillery); thirdly, the materials lost at sea in November 1941 (49,395t) were partially replaced between December 1941 and January 1942, by French deliveries from Tunisia and Algeria, of at least 22,000t of food and gasoline as Vichy was, during that period, in full accordance with Berlin, believing the war with the USSR would soon conclude with peace with Moscow and German victory in Europe; finally, the total weapons lost at sea between 1 August 1941 and 18 January 1942 was: 12 field guns, 67 anti-tank guns, 25 0.787in AA MGs, 338 trucks and 46 tanks (all lost on 23 January 1942 and replaced in May, being all Italian M14/41). These were the weapons for the Italian Division 'Sabratha', which had been reconstructed, but had not

Bay of Suda, November 1941. The torpedo boat *Cassiopea* is refuelling from the stranded full-load British tanker *Eleonora Maersk* (10,694 gross tons). A blessing, given the shortage of fuel oil suffered by the Axis navies in the Mediterranean during autumn 1941. (AC)

been included in the planned offensive in Cyrenaica as its task was only to guard the Tunisian frontier. The division became combat-ready by new deliveries in February 1942.

The British (and later American) war against Axis tonnage often cost the attackers dearly, and was not always a success, notwithstanding numerous claims to the contrary. On 10 June 1940, the Axis had available 2,101,492t of Italian shipping and 203,513t of German freighters to give a total of 2,305,005t. Throughout the war, new ship construction and seizures from Yugoslavia, Greece, France and Britain kept Axis tonnage afloat. On 8 September 1943, the figures were respectively 1,860,777t for the Italians and 263,776t for the Germans (a total of 2,124,553t), not considering some further 100,000 Axis tons in the Black Sea, which opened again to Mediterranean commerce from April 1941 after the surrender of Greece. Throughout the same period, the Allies sank 1,669,707 Axis tons in the Mediterranean, losing little more than 1.7 million tons of their own shipping in the process.

Between 11 June 1940 and 8 September 1943, the Italian shipping loss rate – taking into account all routes, civilian included, and all fronts and areas that had to be kept supplied in the Mediterranean and the Black Sea – was 0.8 per cent, a figure comparable to the 0.7 per cent Captain Roskill submits for the British escorted trade convoys 1939–45 in *The Navy at War*.

Within this picture, the little more than 1.2 million tons of shipping sunk or captured by the Italian Navy[12] (not considering the French merchant vessels found in France and Tunisia in November 1942) amounted to just 10 per cent of the German successes over the same period but the RM score was comparable to the contemporary Japanese total. However, with respect to Italian interests, these losses had a disproportionate impact at the time. If we consider the progress of the Battle of the Atlantic between mid-December 1942 (when the Allies lost their original hopes to rapidly conquer Tunisia and thus open the Mediterranean again) and early June 1943, when British codebreakers read Dönitz's order of 24 May 1943 which stated he was temporarily withdrawing U-boats from the North Atlantic in the face of the new Allied ASW tactics and weapons, the disruption was most certainly effective.

Furthermore, on 29 March 1943, the British government had, indeed, to accept American terms imposing a single pool of Allied merchant shipping, dominated by Washington, thus passing the leadership of the 'strange alliance' – born almost by chance in 1941 – to the USA. This was the price of British logistical and financial dependence upon the United States, with stocks of imported food and raw materials at home now almost running out.

That day, the Italian war, at least according to the dominant thinking in Rome, had a change of values: from a feared, vindictive British peace to the

---

12 The Italian Air Force sank less than 100,000gwt. About 2,000,000gwt were also damaged, to a more or less serious degree, by RM and RA in the Atlantic and Indian Ocean, the Mediterranean and the Red Sea between June 1940 and May 1943.

much more manageable Americans, generally on good terms with Italy since the late 19th century. Their overwhelming power had materialized first-hand in November 1942 with the landings in French North Africa, and victories in Tunisia in May 1943 and Sicily two months later.

The Rest of 1940

On 19 July 1940, in the action off Cape Spada, a brief sortie into the Aegean Sea by two Italian first generation Condottieri cruisers to disrupt the British trade in that area, HMAS *Sydney* hit the cruiser *Colleoni* twice which was then sunk by two torpedoes fired by British destroyers. *Bande Nere*, *Sydney* and *Havock* all experienced minor gunnery damage.

Confident the British would no longer interfere in the Central Mediterranean, on 27 July, Supermarina sent the biggest convoy of the war to Libya, named 'TVL' (*Trasporto Veloce e Lento*: fast and slow transport as there were two convoys) formed of nine freighters. It arrived safely, but the port's congestion demonstrated that only a small, daily convoy could be unloaded in a workable manner.

On 1 August, Mussolini refused Cavagnari's proposal to convert the liners *Rex* and *Conte di Savoia* into fast (26kt) carriers, razing their superstructures. These huge ships would have been very vulnerable to underwater attacks and had, according to the Italian Minister of Communications, a high commercial value. Only the old liner *Roma* was available and so the RM began a new study to convert her into a fast carrier inspired by the British *Ark Royal*, using the almost completed machinery of two light cruisers of the Capitani Romani class whose construction had been stopped in June 1940.

Italian navy intelligence broke the information on 4 August that *Hood* had been damaged on 1 August by a bomb which had struck the bridge front without detonating. The battlecruiser, worn out and unable to do more than 22kt, would soon sail for Britain. Just over a week later, on 13 August, the codebreakers discovered that *Royal Sovereign* had left the Mediterranean for repairs and refit at Durban.

On 15 August, five recently activated RA S.M.79 torpedo bombers attacked, without result, the Mediterranean Fleet at Alexandria. The base was judged too well defended and the two weapons launched got stuck in the mud. Two days later, the Mediterranean Fleet shelled the still-undefended town of Bardia, Libya. Cunningham wrote that the enemy's skill in dispersing motor transports and stores over wide areas of desert rendered this type of operation unjustifiable. That day, the Comando Supremo recorded one dead and some motorbikes damaged. With the value of this tactic proved, Italian forces would always disperse their supplies over the following years.

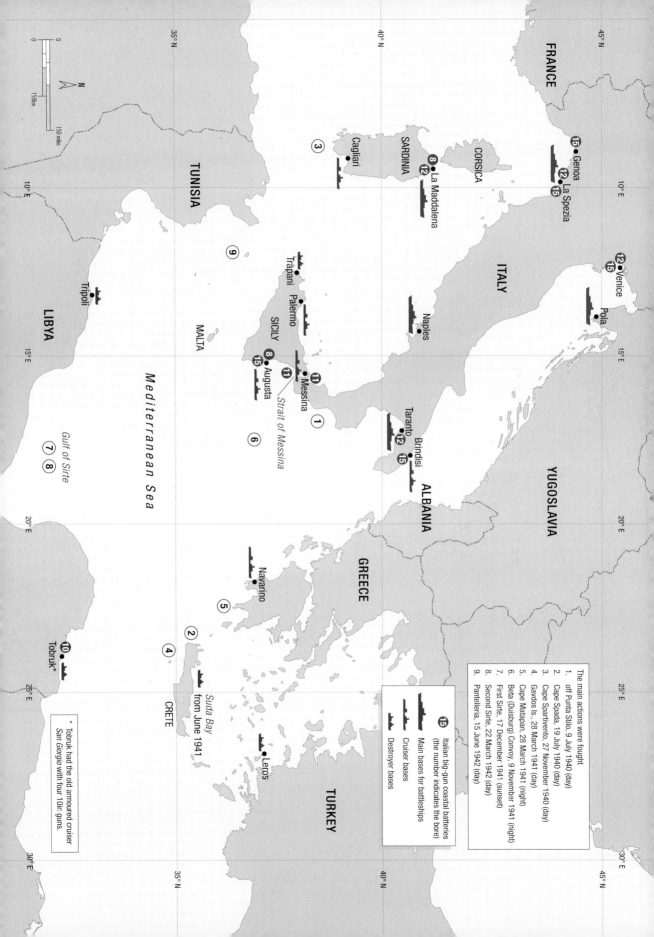

FRANCE

ITALY

CORSICA

SARDINIA

Cagliari

● **15** Genoa
● **12** La Spezia
● **15**

8 La Maddalena
12

3

TUNISIA

9

Trapani ●
Palermo ●
SICILY
8 Augusta
15
11 Messina
11

Naples ●

12 Venice ●
15

Pola ●
12
15

YUGOSLAVIA

Tripoli ●

LIBYA

MALTA

Strait of Messina

1

6

Taranto ●
12
Brindisi ●
15

ALBANIA

GREECE

Mediterranean Sea

Gulf of Sirte
7
8

Navarino ●
5

CRETE
4
2
Suda Bay from June 1941

Leros ●

TURKEY

Tobruk* ●
10

The main actions were fought
1. off Punta Stilo, 9 July 1940 (day)
2. Cape Spada, 19 July 1940 (day)
3. Cape Spartivento, 27 November 1940 (day)
4. Gavdos Is., 28 March 1941 (day)
5. Cape Matapan, 28 March 1941 (night)
6. Beta (Duisburg) Convoy, 9 November 1941 (day)
7. First Sirte, 17 December 1941 (night)
8. Second Sirte, 22 March 1942 (day)
9. Pantelleria, 15 June 1942 (day)

15 Italian big-gun coastal batteries
(the number indicates the bore)

Main bases for battleships

Cruiser bases

Destroyer bases

* Tobruk had the old armoured cruiser
San Giorgio with four 10in guns.

N

0   150km
0   150 miles

On 21 August, FAA Swordfish sank the submarine *Iride* in the Gulf of Bomba, Libya. In the first operation of the Italian navy special attack craft force, later named X MAS Flotilla, *Iride* had been due to mount an SLC human torpedo attack against the Mediterranean Fleet at Alexandria.

Having just arrived at Alexandria on 10 September, the captain of the carrier *Illustrious* proposed a night raid against the Italian battlefleet at Taranto. *Illustrious* had recently delivered new night cockpits to Egypt for the Swordfish torpedo-bombers and advanced auxiliary tanks which allowed take-off from the nearby Greek Ionian islands. The attack would be based on air reconnaissance from Malta by the recently arrived, fast two-engined Martin Maryland bombers. The operation was scheduled for 21 October by *Illustrious* and *Eagle*.

A new SLC attack against Alexandria, this time by the submarine *Gondar*, was aborted on 29 September because the Mediterranean Fleet was at sea. The day after, the boat was sunk by British and Australian destroyers supported by an RAF Sunderland flying boat. The same day, the submarine *Sciré* received the order to cancel a similar operation against Gibraltar when 50 miles from the target, as the always-busy Force H was away.

On 14 October, Italian S.M.79 bombers damaged the carrier *Eagle*. Only *Illustrious* would attack Taranto with just 24 instead of 30 originally planned Swordfish. Only one aircraft – which would miss its target – was thus reserved for *Veneto*.

THE WILD GOOSE CHASES: AUGUST / SEPTEMBER 1940

On the afternoon of 9 July 1940, after the Action off Calabria, Admiral Cunningham was waiting for the reinforcements he had asked for for the Mediterranean Fleet: at least two up-to-date modernized battleships, one more fleet carrier, heavy cruisers and much more. The idea, cultivated since 1937, of a knockout blow through a decisive battle for control of the Mediterranean was over. The RM's battleline was reinforced, with much propaganda, in August 1940, with the addition of three battleships. However, this reinforcement was a bluff as training and, above all, the new 15in guns' teething problems, would continue until early November 1940. The distances between Taranto and Alexandria, the problems of the Italian naval air reconnaissance (too few floatplanes with no night capabilities until January 1942) and the RM's destroyer range did not allow for a timely sortie that would intercept the British battleforce. But confrontations did happen on 31 August 1940 and on 30 September 1940. During the first episode at 1815hrs, two Cavours, seven cruisers and eight destroyers were sighted 140 miles north-west by a Swordfish from *Eagle*. Admiral Cunningham turned south with his two battleships, one carrier, five cruisers and 13 destroyers, waiting for the night and close to a convoy (three transports and four destroyers) bound for Malta. After the war, he stated that his air reconnaissance had signalled five Italian battleships. The Italian line was actually four battleships, two of them not yet truly operational (the purpose of this bluff being to avoid a shore bombardment of Southern Italy or the shelling of the important harbour of Benghazi). No night search from either side was attempted in spite of the British advantage in terms of range and training, and no surface attack developed, only some bomb damage to the merchant vessel *Cornwall* and the Polish destroyer *Garland*. On 30 September, the episode was repeated after a Swordfish from *Illustrious* sighted five Italian battleships 116 miles away. Only *Warspite* sustained splinter damage and casualties, off Sidi Barrani, by bombs dropped by 18 S.M.79 bombers from Rhodes.

MALTA

SICILY

ITALY

Adriatic Sea

Mediterranean Sea

A

116 miles

B

1

140 miles

2

GREECE

The submarine *Scirè* launched her three SLCs towards the Rock on 29 October. Teething troubles with the engines of the underwater attack craft compromised the mission. Only one 'pig' made it into harbour, and was 75yds from *Barham* when it sank, exploding harmlessly a few hours later. *Barham* joined the Mediterranean Fleet on 11 November 1940.

Taranto and its Aftermath

On 6 November, the two Littorios were considered combat-ready. They were going to sail, on 12 November, with the battleforce to cover a bombardment of the Bay of Suda by heavy cruisers. The operation was cancelled after the FAA raid against Taranto on 11 November.

The operation in Taranto was helped by Italy's lack of anti-torpedo nets to protect its battleships. It had been discovered, on 20 June, that the British had effective net cutters able to penetrate World War I single nets, and that double-netting, or new, more robust nets, would not be available before spring 1941, both because the industry could not deliver the new materials in time and because of lack of tugs. The overhead balloon barrage had mostly been blown away some days before by a sudden strong wind and the Italian Army (responsible for their maintenance) had been unable to replace them. Despite a timely warning before the raid, the FAA torpedo bombers from *Illustrious* were able to hit *Cavour*, *Duilio* and *Littorio*. The British assessment the day after was that the first would need one year to be repaired and the other two six months.

Despite the availability by mid-November of five battleships and two carriers, the Mediterranean Fleet did not try to force another fleet action. Britain was too weak and overstretched in 1940–41 to win in the Mediterranean by brute force and as General Sir John Dill, Chief of the Imperial General Staff, said, Britain had to stake everything on an indirect approach, trying to topple Mussolini and, by domino effect, his German counterpart.

The Italian *Vittorio Veneto*, then the most modern and powerful battleship in the world, sailed with *Cesare* and *Doria* on 12 November for Naples. They would remain there until their new anti-torpedo boxes were ready at Taranto from late spring 1941. However, the undamaged battleships were not husbanded. On 17 November, Force H was on a mission to supply new aircraft to Malta. After its carrier-based air reconnaissance discovered the Italian battleforce (*Veneto* and *Cesare*) steaming to intercept them, Somerville decided to launch 14 aircraft towards Malta and retire. Being too far, nine of them crashed at sea or were shot down.

Cape Spartivento (*Capo Teulada*)

On 27 November, *Vittorio Veneto* and *Cesare*, with six heavy cruisers and 14 destroyers, fought a long-range action against Force H (the battleships *Renown*, flagship of Vice-Admiral Somerville, *Ramillies*, carrier *Ark Royal*, five cruisers and 14 destroyers)) escorting a convoy (three motor vessels)) bound for

Malta and Alexandria and protected by two light cruisers, two destroyers and four corvettes.

It was a one-hour affair. At first, the opposing cruisers engaged and the heavy cruiser *Berwick* sustained two 8in direct hits disabling X turret; the light cruiser *Southampton* was seen straddled, sustaining splinter damage and hauling to starboard. According to a signal intercepted at 1337hrs, but decrypted by the Italians only the day after, *Southampton* informed *Renown* that she was able to do only 12.5kt, a circumstance not confirmed by the British version. *Renown* arrived at flank speed, 27kt, leaving behind the outranged *Ramillies* at 20.7kt, to sustain the RN scouting force of Admiral Lancelot Holland. Her shooting caused near-miss damage to the cruiser *Bolzano*'s rudder. When *Renown* and the remaining four British cruisers were within range of *Vittorio Veneto*'s 15in guns, the Italian battleships fired seven salvos at 1305hrs, with turret 3, observing that they twice hit, at 1308hrs, the bow of the second enemy ship of the line (*Renown*). Both sides disengaged. Somerville at 1309hrs because, according to the official report, there was not a chance of engaging the fast Italian vessels. Campioni at 1310hrs because, according to the information broadcast at noon by Supermarina, air reconnaissance had wrongly reported the presence of three RN battleships. A CANT Z.501 land-based flying boat signalled, at 1320hrs, a fire on the bow of a slow-moving British battleship, but this news was broadcast from Rome to Campioni only two hours later. At 1445hrs, ten Italian S.M.79 bombers attacked without results, Force H observing the fire reported previously by the CANT.

Later, on 29 November, the Italian coastwatchers based at Algeciras informed Supermarina that a Kent-class cruiser (*Berwick*) had been docked (Dock 2) with damage at her stern. On 30 November, it was the turn of *Renown* to enter Dock 1 for a week at Gibraltar with damages on her bow and a glancing blow against turret A. HUMINT (Spanish workers in Gibraltar) confirmed the damages to HMS *Renown* were caused by two direct shell hits, one of them a partially detonated one, on both sides which were repaired within two weeks.

The British version recorded only the direct hits on *Berwick*. The 18th Cruiser Squadron War Diary adds *Manchester* at 1332hrs. No mention is made about *Renown*, and *Southampton* was repaired at Durban in December 1940. The Italian destroyer *Lanciere*, slowed by a previous machinery defect, was hit twice (one of them a dud) by HMS *Newcastle*.

Supermarina's final conclusion was that the Action off Cape Spartivento (*Capo Teulada*) was the litmus test of the RM's long-range gunnery proficiency and advantage over the RN's gunnery – much criticized except for

South of Sardinia, 27 November 1940. British 6in guns shooting against an Italian heavy cruiser. The salvos are closely bunched, but the accuracy is average. British spotting of line and deflection were always considered weak by the Italians during long-range actions. (AC)

the recently modernized RN battleships – proving that Fioravanzo's doctrine about the decisive psychological effect in favour of those able to draw first blood was sound. The convoy to Malta had, however, got through and the general political mood after Taranto favoured the removal of Cavagnari and Somigli and the appointment of Iachino replacing Campioni.

1941

Despite some warning by the RM codebreakers about a pending British action off Vlorë (Albania) and three previous attempts at night ambushes by Italian cruisers and destroyers, on 19 December the battleships of the Mediterranean Fleet were able to conduct a brief, blind night shelling from 26,000yds in the direction of the harbour. Three FIAT CR.42 fighters were damaged on an airstrip.

27 November 1940. The cruiser *Fiume* during the Action off Cape Spartivento. On 29 and 30 November 1940, Italian coastal watchers at Algeciras and HUMINT in Gibraltar signalled the battleship *Renown* as having been damaged fore by two 15in (one of them a partially exploded one) direct hits. She was in Dock 1 while the cruiser *Berwick*, damaged (turret Y) by two 8in shells, was in Dock 2. *Renown*'s temporary repairs were over by mid-December 1940. The RM concluded it was satisfied with its gunnery and had confirmed its upper hand in the Central Mediterranean. (AC)

Bardia, which had been besieged from 13 December 1940, was bombarded on 3 January by *Warspite*, *Valiant* and *Barham*. It was a very brief action as the Italian sailors had increased the elevation of the four 4.7in guns along the coast which had been defending the fortress since mid-August 1940. According to a sailor with *Warspite*: 'Splinters hit the *Barham* and our ship but no serious damage had been done'.

On the morning of 6 January, the breaking of Greek ciphers by RM codebreakers allowed the four destroyers of IX Squadriglia to surprise two of the three Hellenic Army regiments of heavy artillery (French-made 155mm howitzers) on the coastal road near Himarë in Albania, along the decisive front of Vlorë. The movement of the guns had been delayed the night before by a bombardment from two Italian torpedo boats and the destroyers arrived steaming at 32kt. Some RAF bombers tried, with no results, to counterattack the bombarding Italians. That day the Greek Army cancelled its last, desperate offensive towards Vlorë.

On 7 January, Mussolini reneged on his earlier carrier decisions, ordering the conversion of the liner *Roma* into a fleet carrier within 12, or better eight months. However, the RA CoS, General Pricolo, stopped the programme within three weeks, explaining that his air force had no suitable aircraft or the necessary know-how. In Rome, everyone believed that the war would be over after the conquest of Greece and the opening of the Italian maritime route for the Black Sea.

A raid by RAF bombers based in Malta on 8 January caused minor damages to *Cesare*. While smokescreen defences at Naples were improved, the battleforce left for La Spezia.

On 10 January, German and Italian Ju 87 dive bombers seriously damaged the carrier *Illustrious* 60 miles west of Malta. The ship would leave the Mediterranean to be repaired in the USA, and was replaced on 10 March by her twin *Formidable*. With *Eagle* worn out and too vulnerable (retiring from the Mediterranean in April 1941), the Mediterranean Fleet's activity was hampered for two months. The three fast (18kt) landing ships *Glenearn*, *Glengyle* and *Glenroy*, with a brigade of commandos, which were meant to be the spearhead of an invasion first of Pantelleria in late January and, later, of Rhodes, planned since October 1940, consequently had to follow the Cape Route, losing two months.

The damage to *Illustrious* sparked an absurd battleship sortie to intercept her from Liguria on 11 January, which was ordered personally by Mussolini and undone the day after. It was a waste of oil, which was already precious.

Genoa was bombarded on 9 February by Force H (HMS *Renown*, *Malaya* and *Ark Royal* with one cruiser and eight destroyers). Covered by a heavy fog and shooting down immediately the only Italian floatplane which sighted the squadron, Admiral Somerville was able to shell the town. The fog, however, was an obstacle to the ships' aims and no serious damage was achieved. The only ship definitely lost was the *Garaventa*, a training ship for teenage boys. Many of the shells did not explode. The fog was also a problem for the shore batteries.

Poor visibility (3,200–4,300yds) then prevented an encounter with the Italian battleforce (*Veneto*, *Cesare* and *Doria* with three cruisers and ten destroyers), which was still at sea to intercept a supposed raid by the three Glen-class landing ships in Sardinia. Iachino decided not to heed the advice from Supermarina and missed by less than 20 miles the opportunity to engage Force H off Corsica beyond the fog and with very good visibility. The blame for the raid was placed on Admiral Campioni and Supermarina, which was still in its running-in phase.

During a secret meeting in Athens on 12 March, Yugoslavian plotters, in touch with the British SOE intelligence agency since January, were persuaded that the RN, master of the Mediterranean, would steam into the Adriatic Sea to protect their planned revolt against the Axis. After seizing power at home, the generals in Belgrade accordingly activated their plan for a retreat to Dalmatia, waiting for British aid. After the end of the brief Yugoslavian campaign, it turned out this had been a misunderstanding. The small Yugoslavian Navy was all seized by the RM on 17 April 1941, except for a worn-out submarine and two MTBs.

Winter 1940–41. Admiral Angelo Iachino (left), the new commander of the battlefleet, on *Vittorio Veneto*. Behind him is a Ro.43 floatplane, a good aircraft for spotter tasks. In autumn 1942, the three Littorios also embarked one or two Re.2000 fighters. (AC)

Gavdos Island, 28 March 1941. The 15in near-miss which damaged HMS *Orion* and caused some minor flooding. (AC)

At dawn on 26 March, an explosive boat hit HMS *York* at Souda Bay, Crete, and the ship was beached. *York* was the last RN heavy cruiser available for operations in the Mediterranean able to do 30kt. The modernized *Kent* had a similar speed, but had been torpedoed by an S.M.79 bomber on 17 September 1940, and the damage suffered by the 27-knotter *Berwick* two months later at the hands of the Italian heavy cruisers *Trieste* and *Pola* confirmed that the remaining RN heavy cruisers were too slow for the Mediterranean. On 1 May 1941, all efforts to save *York* ceased and the wreck became the favourite target of German bombers during the campaign for Crete. Future battles between opposing scouting forces would always involve Italian 8in guns against British 6in and 5.25in guns until April 1943; a tactical advantage for the RM.

On the night of 21/22 April, the Mediterranean Fleet bombarded the harbour of Tripoli. Two empty freighters were sunk, and there was some splinter damage, but the harbour's efficiency was not affected. A floating mine slightly damaged *Valiant*. A later plan to block Tripoli by scuttling the old target vessel *Centurion* was compromised by the machinery defects of the intended blockship.

An RN squadron of two cruisers and six destroyers had to embark troops at Kalamata on 28 April during the retreat from continental Greece. Italian wireless signals that were intercepted but not decrypted (as the main RM ciphers were unreadable) induced the senior captain to abandon the operation, fearing that he would be engaged the next morning off Crete by Italian cruisers. However, the Italian ships in the area were only occupying Kefalonia. The memory of Gavdos thus caused three-quarters of the British and Imperial POWs to be taken on the mainland of Greece and the loss of the Yugoslavian plotters (about 1,500 officers and their families) from the 27 March Coup.

By 8 May 1941, *Littorio* was back in service at Taranto, and, the day after, *Queen Elizabeth* joined the Mediterranean Fleet, steaming eastward from Gibraltar with the Egypt-bound Operation *Tiger* convoy – the last merchant vessels which would arrive there without taking the Cape route for the following two years. Due to low clouds, fog and rain, Italian air reconnaissance had failed to sight them in time for a sortie by the RM battleforce (*Cesare* and *Doria*) based at Naples. Churchill's ideas about Force H shelling Naples on the way, or basing the battleship at Malta to stop the Axis traffic with Libya, had been discarded by the more prudent First Lord Admiral Sir Dudley Pound.

North of Crete, at 0914hrs on 22 May, the torpedo boat *Sagittario* claimed a torpedo struck the cruiser *Naiad* starboard. The 15th Cruiser Squadron retired immediately and did not attack the slow convoy of motor fishing vessels ferrying German troops, escorted by *Sagittario*. At 0930hrs, Luftwaffe aircraft attacked but had used up their last torpedo the day before.[13] However, Lieutenant Louis E.

North of Crete, 22 May 1941. The torpedo boat *Sagittario* is dodging the British and Australian cruisers' salvos after having fired her two starboard torpedoes. Note the 6in or 5.25 shells did not explode. (AC)

Le Bailly described a torpedo punching a hole through his ship stem and a huge hole port side. Other witnesses[14] and photographic evidence confirm this version. It is another of many unresolvable cases. Steaming at 16kt, the crippled *Naiad* slowed down the squadron and *Warspite* and *Valiant*, patrolling west of Crete to repulse any RM menace, had to enter the Luftwaffe's range of action to support the 15th Cruiser Squadron. Both battleships were damaged by German bombs and *Warspite* departed in June for repairs in the USA.

South of Crete on 27 May, German and Italian bombers damaged the carrier *Formidable*, *Barham* (escorting against RM cruisers) and the destroyer *Nubian*. They all left the Mediterranean to be repaired in the USA, South Africa and India. The same day, three SLCs ferried by the submarine *Sciré* failed to carry out a new attack against Force H at Gibraltar, due to mechanical problems.

On 16 June, the Taranto-damaged battleship *Duilio* returned to service. The next month the Germans withdrew their promises of oil supplies from Romania because the war against the USSR, unleashed by Berlin on 22 June, needed every drop of fuel available. Rome could thus only trust the production of the Italian concession of Ploesti. The first effect of this news was to reduce almost to zero the missions of the modernized RM battleships.

On 8 July, the liner *Roma* began, despite the RA's stubborn opposition, to be converted into a carrier, named *Aquila*, to be completed in February 1942. Unfortunately, in September 1941, Germany's offer of spare equipment from the planned twin of their carrier *Graf Zeppelin* was accepted. This meant that the German trolley and catapult system would be fitted, instead of the original, easier free-take-off method devised by the RM. This compromised the commissioning of the carrier, as did the delays to the arrester wire system. In July 1943, the trials with Re.2001 fighters were still ongoing, with modest success.

13 Schmidt Rudi, *Achtung-Torpedo los!*, Bernhard & Graefe, Koblenz, 1991.
14 Harker, Jack S., *Well Done Leander*, Collins, Auckland, 1971 and Hartfield Hatfield, George, *H.M.A.S. Perth 1939–1941*, Springwood, Faulconbridge, 2009.

Damaged at Cape Matapan by a British torpedo bomber, *Veneto* was back in service on 22 July; a day later, *Renown* was damaged by Italian S.M.79 bombers in the western Mediterranean, her speed restricted to 20kt by torn plating in the starboard bulge. Repairs in Britain would be completed in December 1941.

Barham returned to Alexandria from the repair yard on 15 September. On 20 September, three SLCs launched by the submarine *Sciré* attacked Force H at Gibraltar. RN motor launches repulsed two of them, which later sank a storage hulk and damaged a merchant vessel. The third penetrated the boom, and damaged the tanker *Denbydale* with its mine, trying to set the harbour on fire with the tanker's fuel oil. This attempt failed due to British fuel being of better quality than the Italian one (not to mention the dangerous synthetic German one), with a lower flash point.

November was a costly month for the RN in the Mediterranean. On 13 November, *Ark Royal* was torpedoed by the German submarine U-81 and sank the next day, while on 25 November, *Barham* was torpedoed and sunk by U-331. Given the Italian battleforce threat, the battle squadron of the Mediterranean Fleet had been escorting a cruiser squadron that was to bombard the Halfaya Pass shore road.

However, in the Night Action of Cape Bon, on 13 December 1941, Allied destroyers sank the light cruisers *Di Giussano* and *Da Barbiano*. *Vittorio Veneto* was torpedoed by the submarine HMS *Urge* on 14 December while escorting a convoy to Libya.

THE REALITIES BEHIND SEA POWER: THE FIRST BATTLE OF SIRTE

At a critical moment during the British offensive, Operation *Crusader*, in North Africa, and after brilliant actions by Force K, Italian Navy personnel struck back at sunset on 17 December 1941.

Since June 1941, the RM had had more powerful battleships than the Mediterranean Fleet but they mostly remained in their own waters. The RM's night fighting capabilities, being still without radar sets, had been confirmed obsolete, and sea power was, until 1944, a daylight matter using battleships.

The 17 December 1941 action was a brief, 11-minute engagement before darkness: three Italian battleships, two cruisers and ten destroyers against four RN cruisers and 12 destroyers (one of them Australian and another Dutch) who were escorting the camouflaged tanker *Breconshire*

(which German and Italian air reconnaissance had signalled to be a battleship). *Littorio*'s 15in guns straddled the tanker from 35,000yds with her first half salvo; *Breconshire* turned south at once, escorted by two destroyers laying smoke; RN cruisers gave additional support but were repulsed by Italian shooting and RM destroyer counterattack. 'An image of fantastic beauty in the dusk' wrote Admiral Iachino. One British and one Australian destroyer were damaged. During the following night, the RM's task was to protect an important convoy of German tanks bound to Benghazi. Iachino's well-known ability as a skilled manoeuvrer avoided any British interception. The Italian crews assumed the British were deterred, also at night, by the big guns of their battleships. The RM's 1941 crisis of confidence was over after 40 hard days.

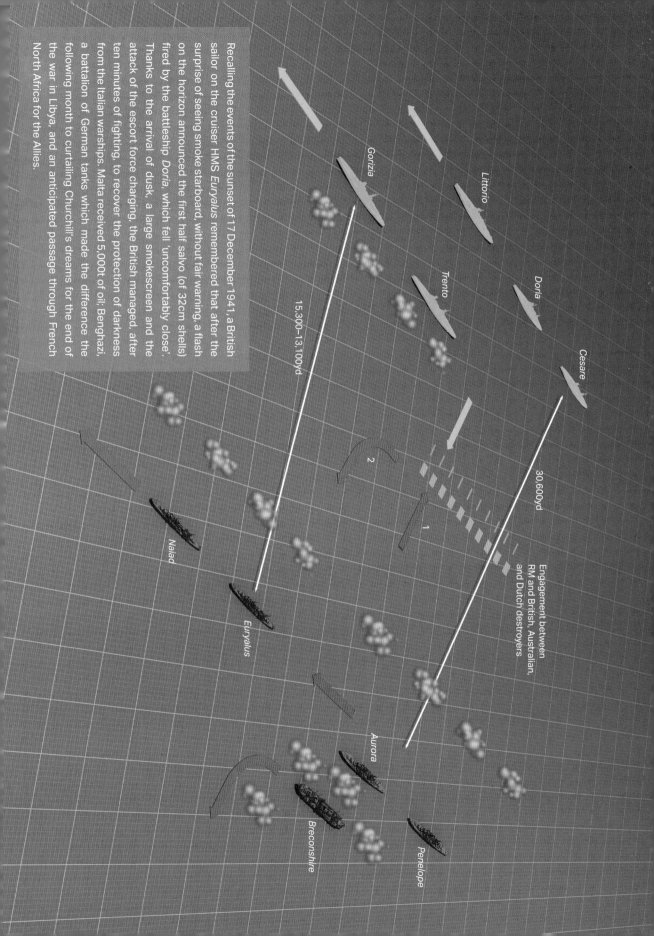

Recalling the events of the sunset of 17 December 1941, a British sailor on the cruiser HMS *Euryalus* remembered that after the surprise of seeing smoke starboard, without fair warning, a flash on the horizon announced the first half salvo (of 32cm shells) fired by the battleship *Doria*, which fell 'uncomfortably close'. Thanks to the arrival of dusk, a large smokescreen and the attack of the escort force charging, the British managed, after ten minutes of fighting, to recover the protection of darkness from the Italian warships. Malta received 5,000t of oil; Benghazi, a battalion of German tanks which made the difference the following month to curtailing Churchill's dreams for the end of the war in Libya, and an anticipated passage through French North Africa for the Allies.

Littorio

Gorizia

Doria

Trento

Cesare

15,300–13,100yd

30,600yd

Engagement between RM and British, Australian, and Dutch destroyers

2

1

Naiad

Euryalus

Aurora

Breconshire

Penelope

North of Crete, 22 May 1941. HMS *Naiad* punctured starboard side by a torpedo launched by *Sagittario* which later exploded opening a 'huge hole' port above, confirmed by the light through the first leak. This accident was denied at first, but confirmed after the war by the then Lt. (E) Louis Le Bailly. (AC)

On 19 December, three SLCs launched off Alexandria by the submarine *Sciré* seriously damaged *Queen Elizabeth* and *Valiant*. The attempt to set the harbour on fire by mining the tanker *Sagona* crippled the ship, but nothing else. Churchill stated: 'six Italians equipped with poor laughable materials, made totter the military balance in the Mediterranean Sea, advantaging the Axis'.

1942

In February, *Duilio* (Admiral Bergamini's flagship) sortied with four cruisers and 11 destroyers to intercept a convoy from Alexandria to Malta (four cruisers, 15 destroyers and three freighters). One of the merchant vessels, damaged by aircraft, went to Tobruk; the other two, hit by the Luftwaffe, were scuttled and the escort force turned back to Egypt.

A similar situation involving a convoy from Alexandria to Malta culminated, on 22 March, in the Second Battle of Sirte. This action marked the evolution of Iachino's principles. The Italian Admiral, considered too young and inexperienced by Cavagnari in 1940, planned the encounter believing, like Gavdos the year before, that the British, heirs to Nelson, would follow the three cruisers and four destroyers of the III Divisione (Admiral Angelo Parona) into a trap, finding themselves surrounded between Parona's ships and the *Littorio* with three further destroyers. The RN force led by Rear-Admiral Philip Vian (four cruisers and 11 destroyers) was careful not to do this, and after a brief long-range exchange came back to escort the convoy (four merchant vessels with a direct escort formed by the old anti-aircraft cruiser *Carlisle* and six Hunt-class destroyers). As a storm was approaching fast, Iachino understood he had no time to duck around the enemy and decided to position his force to cut the route to Malta and engage, until sunset, despite the bad weather, low visibility, and being to leeward of the enemy. His declared purpose was to gain time to give the Axis' bombers the possibility of a lucky shot the next morning and he dared to expose *Littorio*, the only true Italian battleship then available, to within 6,000yds from the

British destroyers, which were behind their own smoke curtain and ready to sortie and launch their torpedoes. The cruisers *Cleopatra* and *Euryalus* and the destroyers *Kingston*, *Legion*, *Havock*, *Sikh* and *Lively* were damaged while *Littorio* was hit by one 4.7in on her starboard aft deck breaking a pair of teak planks. The day after, the convoy sustained a further ordeal from aircraft and mines, so much so that the Governor of Malta lamented to the War Cabinet that only 877t of supplies, including some bicycles, had arrived, of the 32,249t originally shipped. During a storm that night, the Italians lost two destroyers (*Lanciere* and *Scirocco*) and the British recorded, over the following weeks, the loss of the crippled destroyers *Kingston*, *Legion* and *Havock* to bombers and submarines

On 9 May, USS *Wasp* launched Spitfires for Malta with HMS *Eagle*. The US carrier had already conducted a similar operation alone, on 20 April 1942. On 13 May, torpedo-damaged *Vittorio Veneto* returned to service, and the next day the submarine *Ambra* launched three SLCs to attack *Queen Elizabeth* in the floating drydock and the submarine depot ship *Medway*. The action failed.

On 14–16 June, 1942 Iachino, leading *Littorio*, *Vittorio Veneto*, four cruisers and 12 destroyers, confirmed his determination by repulsing the *Vigorous* convoy (seven cruisers and 25 destroyers escorting 11 merchant vessels, the old anti-aircraft cruiser *Coventry*, two rescue vessels, the dummy battleship *Centurion*, four corvettes and two fleet minesweepers) from Alexandria to Malta in spite of many air and submarine attacks. The cruiser *Trento* was torpedoed twice

BEFORE THE BATTLE OF PANTELLERIA, 15 JUNE 1942

(overleaf)

At dawn, relaxation at last on the bridge. The RN's superiority at night was a recognized hard fact by November 1941, and British air attacks during darkness were another clear and present danger from that autumn. The RM night combat doctrine was, in 1940, like that of the British at Jutland, and later hasty improvements were not enough. But when the sun rose, the Italian Navy was always confident about its ability to face the enemy with gunnery, superior speed and maneuverability. During the Action off Pantelleria, on 15 June 1942, Admiral Da Zara, commanding the VII Divisione (cruisers *Eugenio di Savoia* and *Montecuccoli* with five destroyers) made the best use of these qualities, sinking the destroyer *Bedouin*, the tanker *Kentucky* and the freighters *Chant* (torpedoed by the destroyer *Vivaldi*, it exploded one hour later) and *Burdwan*. The old anti-aircraft cruiser *Cairo*, the destroyer *Partridge* and the fleet minesweeper *Hebe*

were damaged by gunfire. The Italians claimed a direct hit on the destroyer *Matchless* too; this incident was denied by the British, but it is confirmed by a clear photo made with the telephoto lens on board *Eugenio* at 0725hrs.

In the illustration, the Ro.43 floatplanes (one for each cruiser) have just been catapulted and, on the Admiral's bridge, Da Zara can enjoy his cup of coffee, a taste any sailor after a long night-watch knows well. According to regulations, the Admiral band rank had to be on the right, not the left side of his *berretto di navigazione* (the service at sea cap), but Da Zara was well known for his non-conformist and unauthorized (*fuori ordinanza*) habits. A riding champion, fluent in English (in his cabin he had an autographed picture of the future Duchess of Windsor, treasured since the 1920s when he commanded a river gunboat in China), he was beloved by his staff and crews.

The Battle of Pantelleria, 15 June 1942. HMS *Bedouin* sinking. Leading a gallant charge against the Italian cruisers, she was damaged (12 direct hits), immobilized and, at last, finished by a Regia Aeronautica S.M.79 torpedo bomber. (AC)

and lost and *Littorio* was hit by a torpedo, while the Axis light forces sunk the cruiser *Hermione*, three destroyers and two freighters. The War Cabinet, somewhat embarrassed, on 22 June ordered the record be 'amend[ed] to show that E. Convoy turned back for lack of fuel'.

Two bad days for the British fleet began when the British carrier *Eagle* was sunk in the Western Mediterranean by the German submarine U-73 on 11 August. The carriers *Furious* and *Victorious* also suffered damage (respectively two days and two and a half months of repairs) after a collision necessary to avoid three torpedoes launched by the Italian submarine *Uarsciek*. The following day the carrier *Indomitable* was severely damaged by German bombers in the Western Mediterranean, and the carrier *Victorious* was hit, with little effect, by an Italian Re.2001 fighter-bomber. *Rodney* was damaged near the Strait of Sicily by an Italian Ju 87 which dropped its bomb abaft her stern before disappearing into the sea.

The night of 12/13 August, Luftwaffe air reconnaissance communicated, mistakenly, that a British battleship and a carrier had rounded Cape Bon. This piece of news and the Luftwaffe's preference to reserve Italians and their own fighters for bomber escort, caused the cancellation of a mission by six Italian cruisers and 11 destroyers to intercept the Pedestal convoy off Pantelleria the next morning. Only five of the total 14 merchant vessels of the convoy arrived at Malta after three days of Axis air, submarine and MTBs attacks. The famous tanker *Ohio* (sunk a few days later due to the damage suffered) wasn't carrying avgas (whose stocks in the besieged island would suffice until December 1942), but fuel oil for a landing from Malta at Sfax (Tunisia), scheduled for November 1942 and annulled because of lack of local sea control a few days before the invasion of French North Africa. Most of the supplies were, indeed ammunition, and the few food and comfort items available were reserved for the garrison and British families. The event had consequences on public opinion as seen in this article published in September 1942 in the *Times of Malta*: 'We have put up with bombing, blasting, nights in uncomfortable shelters, low pay, black market, Victory Kitchens, lack of electric lighting, lack of buses, lack of meat, lack of milk, restricted rations with little grumbling, but what is the last straw is the evidence of preferential treatment'.

The new battleship *Roma* joined La Squadra at Taranto on 22 August. Four days later, *Littorio* completed her repairs following the torpedo damage which had occurred on the night of 15/16 June 1942.

Allied Landings Begin

Operation *Torch* began on 8 November. The American and British landings in French North Africa were protected in the Mediterranean by *Duke of York, Nelson,*

Rodney and *Renown*, and the carriers *Victorious*, *Formidable* and *Furious* against a possible sortie of the French battleship *Strasbourg* (the MN *Forces de haute mer* was the only battleforce which could react in time in the Western Mediterranean). After the French armistice was signed in North Africa on 11 November, *Nelson*, *Rodney* and the carrier *Formidable* moved

The Battle of Pantelleria, 15 June 1942. HMS *Matchless* on fire photographed from *Montecuccoli*. The RN official report and narratives stated there was no damage whatsoever. (AC)

intermittently between Gibraltar, Mers-el-Kébir and Algiers thwarting, during the first half of 1943, the RM plans for a craft attack operation against them using new MTR explosive boats ferried by the submarine *Ambra*. The British believed they had repulsed, on 23 March 1943, an attack by 'pigs' at Mers-el-Kébir, but it was a false alarm.

The three Littorios moved from Taranto to Naples on 12 November, hoping for a German supply of oil which would not materialize because the Soviets had attacked unexpectedly on the Eastern Front on 19 November, encircling Stalingrad four days later.

A USAAF raid over Naples on 4 December caused the loss of the light cruiser *Muzio Attendolo*, and damage to *Raimondo Montecuccoli* and *Eugenio*. The battleforce would leave two days later for the much better protected base of La Spezia. Geographically, the range from Algiers was always the same, but the confirmed lack of oil would compromise any offensive move both by the battleships and the two heavy cruisers *Gorizia* and *Trieste* now based at La Maddalena.

Having conducted two successful operations by frogmen on 14 July and 15 September against the merchant vessels in the anchorage outside Gibraltar, a new attack was made on 9 December by three SLCs against Force H inside the harbour. The operation failed and only MV *Forest* was slightly damaged. Two further successful attacks were made on 8 May and 4 August 1943 against the freighters moored off the harbour.

On 30 December, *Cesare* whose electrical system had been made in 1936 with autarchic materials as a consequence of sanctions (aluminium for copper and resins for mica isolators), was sent to Pola to serve as a gunnery training ship. She had to be replaced, according to the programme, in May 1943 by *Cavour*, cabled in autumn 1942 from scratch with better materials.

RM staff still believed the war would be won in North Africa, as the Germans had promised powerful divisions and supplies for the new front in Tunisia with its large harbours and facilities at Bizerte and Tunis. Accordingly, a document rich in wishful thinking was sent on 14 January to Mussolini about plans to expand the RM. For the moment, there was no fuel except for destroyers, but once the Maikop oil production was reactivated or, better, a separate peace with the USSR signed, by 1944 the RM battleforce would

Rome, spring 1943. Mussolini, Grossadmiral Dönitz and, standing up, General Ambrosio, Chief of the *Comando Supremo*. On 12 May 1943, it was confirmed that it was impossible for La Squadra to act east and south of Sicily. (AC)

be able to field four Littorios and three modernized battleships. In 1946, these would be strengthened by the addition of the two former French Dunkerques, scuttled at Toulon on 27 November 1942, but then refloated and repaired. The fleet carrier *Aquila* would be joined, in 1944, by the similar *Sparviero* (former liner *Augustus*) as new, powerful diesel engines would be available at last. Two light carriers, the former heavy cruisers *Bolzano* and the French *Foch* (also scuttled at Toulon) would follow in 1945–46. However, on 29 January Mussolini changed his mind about any expansion. He and King Victor Emmanuel III believed the war would be over, one way or another, in 1943, as Italy could not sustain a longer period of warfare.

On 10 April, the first long-range USAAF raid was made against La Maddalena (which is often subject to strong winds, compromising any smokescreen), sinking the cruiser *Trieste* and severely damaging *Gorizia* on the eve of a raid by III Divisione against some small convoys going from Algiers to Bône. From this point onwards, the opposing scouting forces were on equal (6in gun) terms.

This was followed, on 14 April, by the first of a series of raids against La Spezia by Bomber Command and the USAAF. Surrounded by hills, the base was a difficult target. The RAF also studied an attack using bouncing bombs.

Admiral Dönitz, the new commander-in-chief of the German Navy since 30 January 1943, told Mussolini on 12 May, during a meeting in Rome, that the Italian battleforce could not engage the enemy east of Sicily, as since August 1942 the area had been dominated by the RAF's electronic superiority. It would be left to the Axis armies and air forces to stop an Allied landing along the beaches. It was also confirmed that the submarine war by conventional boats was lost, until the planned, revolutionary new electric U-Boot could be commissioned. Allied trade would suffer only sporadic losses for the rest of the war.

Another USAAF raid on 5 June damaged *Veneto* (repaired by 1 July) and *Roma*, which returned to service on 13 August. However, between May and July 1943, the USN had sent the modern battleships *Alabama* and *South Dakota* to Scapa Flow, allowing *Warspite*, *Valiant*, *Nelson*, *Rodney* and the carrier *Indomitable* to leave Britain on 23 June to join *King George V*, *Howe* (at Gibraltar since May 1943) and the fleet carrier *Formidable* in the Western Mediterranean. Any enduring Italian hope to pit their battleforce against the enemy armada was thus relinquished.

Landings in Italy

The Allied landings in Sicily began on 10 July 1943. At noon, Mussolini decided not to send the battlefleet (*Littorio* and *Vittorio Veneto* with six light cruisers and 11 destroyers) against the six battleships and two fleet carriers (not to mention 15 cruisers, 128 destroyers, three monitors, 83 escort vessels, 243 British MTBs, MGBs and MMS, and US Navy PTs (comprising 1,742 landing ships and craft and 342 merchant vessels). An action off Augusta on the afternoon of 11 July would be too late as British armoured cars and tanks were by then rolling towards the 12-mile-long naval line defending Augusta from the rear.

At Taranto, only the cruiser *Cadorna* and the destroyer *Nicoloso Da Recco* were available, as the fuel for *Duilio* and *Doria* would arrive from Bari on 20 July and these two modernized battleships would only be able to do their first training sortie, after one year moored with skeleton crews, on 27 July. The Axis air forces, with merely 200 attack aircraft in flying condition over Sicily during the first week of the invasion and much less later, could barely achieve pinpricks.

However, RA Re.2002 dive bombers claimed *Nelson* damaged by three near-miss bombs on 13 July.[15] *Nelson* had gone to Malta that day to repair minor damage to some tubes of her superheater. On 16 July, the carrier *Indomitable* was torpedoed and seriously damaged at night by a S.M.79 torpedo bomber. On 20 July, German bombers made, unbeknown to the Italians, a night raid against the British battleships and carriers now at Malta using, for the first time, their secret guided bombs. They scored no results. The attack was repeated on the night of 25/26 July, still without success.

The US Army occupied Messina on 17 August 1943, and the campaign for Sicily was over. The next day the carriers *Illustrious* and *Unicorn* arrived at Gibraltar. They were followed by the American-built RN escort carriers *Attacker*, *Battler*, *Hunter* and *Stalker*, which would, along with HMS *Unicorn*, make available Seafire fighters for a British landing at Crotone, Calabria, scheduled for September. In October it would be time for an American landing in southern Sardinia, followed by a further invasion, to be supported later by French reinforcements in Corsica. *King George V* and *Howe* would be replaced for the October landings by the battleships *Queen Elizabeth* and *Richelieu*.

On 19 August, the USN carrier *Ranger* replaced *Illustrious* at Scapa Flow, which in turn would substitute *Indomitable* in the Mediterranean. The brand-new USN battleship *Iowa* was sent to Newfoundland, arriving on 27 August, allowing the RN to keep the two King George Vs in the Mediterranean until October 1943.

An attack against an Italian battleship at Taranto by a single Chariot (the British version of the Italian 'pigs') ferried by the submarine *Ultor* was cancelled on 28 August because the planned Allied landing at Crotone had just been hurriedly replaced by a new invasion at Salerno. *Ultor* was scheduled to launch her Chariot off Spezia, but the Armistice would be announced before it could take place. Meanwhile the X MAS Flotilla was organizing a desperate full attack,

---

15 Iain Ballantyne recorded interviews about this.

During summer 1943, it was impossible for La Squadra to fight for East Sicily (not to mention southern Sicily). Only Sea Denial using fast coastal forces and submarines was possible – naval guerrilla warfare without much strategic effect. This is one of the 60t MS 'motosiluranti' introduced by the RM from August 1942, replacing the smaller (24t) and less seaworthy MAS.

at dawn, scheduled for October, against one battleship based at Gibraltar by the combined action of new types of surface and underwater attack craft.

On 3 September, a British and Canadian corps landed in Calabria and advanced slowly north. Under the double Allied and German threat, Italy had to sue for an armistice. The battlefleet was ready to sail on 8 September against the Allied landing force directed towards Salerno. Smelling a rat, Admiral Raffaele de Courten, the new Minister and CoS of the Navy after the fall of Mussolini, ordered the battleforce to sail at once, giving up the air cover by the RA and Luftwaffe scheduled for 9 September. General Vittorio Ambrosio, leader of the *Comando Supremo* from 1 February 1943, replacing Cavallero, and the mastermind of the fall of Mussolini and of the Armistice with the Allies, twice ordered at noon it not to leave La Spezia. In the afternoon, after King Victor Emmanuel III decided, against the advice of his counsellors, to confirm the Armistice signed five days before by the new Prime Minister Marshal Badoglio, the agreement between Italy and the Allies was confirmed worldwide at 1947hrs.

For La Squadra it was a shock. The first reaction was to scuttle everywhere and De Courten was forced to impose himself on Bergamini. The Secretary of State, Cordell Hull, wrote in his memoirs:

In line with this thought, the surrender of Italy the following month, although ostensibly on an unconditional basis, was actually, as I have previously mentioned, a negotiated surrender, and the terms of the Armistice were agreed to in discussions in Lisbon, Portugal, between representatives of the Anglo-American Combined Chiefs of Staff and Marshal Badoglio.

The End of the War

General Eisenhower, Supreme Allied Commander in the Mediterranean, and Cunningham, Commander-In-Chief of Allied Naval Forces in the MTO (Mediterranean Theatre of Operations) since 8 November 1942, decided from the beginning not to ask for humiliating conditions for the RM's fate. For their part, Supermarina and Bergamini refused to follow Allied instructions about the transfer of the Italian warships and merchant vessels in Anglo-American-controlled harbours. The battleforce thus sailed from La Spezia and Genoa, early on 9 September, for La Maddalena; it was a case of wait and see. The common opinion was the Germans would leave southern and central Italy and the European war would be over, anyway, within some weeks with the fall of Hitler. *Doria* and *Duilio* had to stay at Taranto and *Cesare* sailed for

Cattaro, in Dalmatia. On 9 September, at 1000hrs, a false report about German paratroopers advancing unopposed towards Taranto induced Admiral Fioravanzo, then commander of the local naval department, to persuade Da Zara not to scuttle his squadron, but to sail for Malta, explaining that as long as he had the control of his armed warships, ready to be scuttled at any time with the Italian flag not hauled down, nothing would be compromised, while the destruction of the fleet would have given the British that

Naples, 26 June 1942. Mussolini on the cruiser *Montecuccoli* after the sweeping surface victory of Pantelleria. Admiral Da Zara is on the right; the CoS of the navy, Admiral Riccardi, behind the dictator. In front of Il Duce is the young secretary of the party, Aldo Vidussoni. (AC)

total victory they had vainly pursued during the war. Da Zara accepted and his little force (two battleships, two unprotected cruisers and a lone destroyer) left in the afternoon. They were attacked, without damages, by a few German Fw 190 fighter-bombers and the Italian anti-aircraft guns replied.

The battleforce that left La Spezia had a much more tragic ending. Some islands of the La Maddalena archipelago were occupied by German commandos (*Küstenjäger*) at noon on 9 September. Supermarina informed Bergamini, and La Squadra changed course to sail outside the Strait of Bonifacio. It was attacked, soon after, by German bombers armed with guided weapons. It was the first time that high-altitude bombing had been effective in the Mediterranean against warships manoeuvring at high speed. In spite of AA fire, *Roma*, Bergamini's flagship, was hit twice and sunk and her sister ship *Italia* (former *Littorio*) was damaged. Bergamini died, along with all his staff. The new commander of the battleforce, Admiral Romeo Oliva, turned south that night.

On 10 September, Da Zara, escorted by *King George V*, arrived at Malta. The British sent boarding parties, but the Italians did not allow them to access below decks or to touch the wireless antennas. An uneasy balance was established and the night and day after passed without trouble, helped by the politeness of the British sailors who had orders to avoid incidents. The next day the main Italian battleforce sighted *Warspite*, *Valiant* and seven destroyers. The courteous behaviour of the Allied crews, quite different from the jeers that had greeted the German fleet at Scapa Flow on 21 November 1918, diffused the tension. Oliva's warships arrived at Malta a few hours later, this time with no boarding parties. In the afternoon, there was a meeting between Da Zara (the senior RM officer at Malta) and Cunningham. The Italian admiral was greeted with full military honours. Cunningham accepted Da Zara's word about respect of the Armistice terms and the five boarding parties were withdrawn at sunset. On 12 September, as the Kingdom of Italy reacted to German aggression unleashed a quarter of an hour after the broadcast confirming the Armistice, the Allies asked Da Zara to send two RM destroyers to Corsica to ferry munitions plus American troops to the

Malta, 11 September 1943. HMS *Warspite* sailors according the honours of war to Admiral Da Zara, commander of La Squadra. A never forgotten act of loyalty quite different from the German surrenders in November 1918 and May 1945. (AC)

Italian Army fighting the Germans there. The proposal was accepted at once. Cunningham, a loyal adversary and a man of common sense, wrote on 14 September: 'I am quite convinced that all the ships are prepared to scuttle should things not be to their liking'.

In fact, a tug-of-war was going on between Roosevelt and Churchill about the fate of the Italian battleforce. The British wanted to seize it, to tropicalize the two Littorios and to send them, flying the White Ensign, to the Pacific to politically balance the American dominance there since the beginning of the war with Japan. The USA preferred to have the battleships in the South Pacific with Italian flags and crews.[16] Their short range would matter less, as similarly short-legged British warships found refuelling and resupplying at sea practical in the Pacific in 1944–45.

King Victor Emmanuel and De Courten would welcome such a use for La Squadra and, in October 1943, Admiral Louis Hamilton, Flag Officer in Malta, told Da Zara the Littorios, with the Italian flag, would sail to the USA to be refitted (radar sets, new anti-aircraft batteries and directors) for the South Pacific to act as battlecruisers for the old USN battleships, while the two Duilios would join, as RM ships, the British Eastern Fleet. King Victor Emmanuel asked in return for an immediate peace treaty, granting his kingdom the 1922 borders. It was too high a political price, and as a result, Italy limited itself to declaring war on Germany as a cobelligerent on 13 October. On 16 October, *Veneto* and *Italia* were thus confined in the Great Bitter Lake, in the Suez Canal, until February 1947. The American request was renewed in mid-October 1944, and the new government led by Prime Minister Ivanoe Bonomi[17] asked again for the terms of the year before, but with the same outcome.

In June 1945, the new Italian government, led after the end of the war in Europe by Ferruccio Parri, a partisan leader who trusted in American goodwill after the US Army had removed Tito's troops from Trieste, Gorizia, Pola and Monfalcone and sent back the French after the Germans retreated from the Alps on 23 April 1945. Parri accepted without pre-conditions to declare war on Japan (15 July 1945) and to send the battlefleet to join the Eastern Fleet, where the sloop *Eritrea* and the destroyer *Carabiniere* had been serving since September 1943 (France had, during summer 1945, two destroyers and the *Richelieu* stationed there). This decision was never put into practice due to the end of the conflict in the Pacific in August 1945.

---

16 It was one of the many Allied leaders' fancies, like the Alaskas large cruisers built to answer the non-existent Japanese pocket battleship threat or Churchill's idea to complete, in Britain, the French battleship *Jean Bart*.

17 The previous PM Badoglio, a lone, very ambitious man considered too submissive towards the British, had been sacked, in June 1944, by the Crown and the new democratic Italian parties.

ANALYSIS

The RM battleforce had been conceived to control the Ionian Sea and the Strait of Sicily. This aim was achieved until the Allied conquest of Tunisia, in May 1943, and of Sicily the following August.

Supermarina never failed to see what mattered and executed its strategies sensibly and clinically in order to win the naval war by 'bleeding white the Red Ensign', or to facilitate a land victory by enabling the Army to conquer the Suez Canal or, briefly in 1943, to support an advance from Tunisia to Morocco. Plans for the invasion of Malta, a materially impossible task in 1940–41 in front of the British coastal defences, were prepared in 1941–42, but in June 1942 the Germans refused their indispensable support.

The basic instrument of the Italian battleforce, the battleships, worked well. Except for the delayed recommissioning of *Cavour*, damaged by a magnetic pistol torpedo, the protection of the other battleships, mainly the Littorios, proved solid. The RM's supposed excessive gunnery dispersion is merely a myth. The numbers speak for themselves.

During the seven major surface day actions fought between the Royal Navy and the Regia Marina (night actions were dictated by different logic and tactics), the direct hits, number of shells fired and confirmed near-misses from the officially recognized records are as follows:

DIRECT HITS

Battle	Regia Marina Ships Hit	Royal Navy Ships Hit
Calabria	*Cesare* (one 15in), *Bolzano* (three 6in)	
Cape Spada	*Colleoni* (two 6in), *Bande Nere* (two 4.7in)	*Sydney* (one 6in)
Cape Spartivento	*Lanciere* (two 6in)	*Berwick* (two 8in)
Second Sirte	*Littorio* (one 4.7in)	*Cleopatra* (one 6in), *Euryalus* (one 15in), *Kingston* (one 8in)
Pantelleria	*Montecuccoli* (one 4.7in), *Eugenio* (one 4.7in), *Vivaldi* (one 4.7in)	*Cairo* (one 6in; one 5.512in), *Bedouin* (11 6in; one 4.7in), *Partridge* (three 6in), *Hebe* (one 6in)
Total hits, confirmed by both sides	RM 24	RN 14
Warships damaged*	Italian 9	British 9

*Two warships, both unprotected, were immobilized by shells and finished by torpedoes: *Colleoni* and *Bedouin*.

NUMBER OF SHELLS FIRED

	Italian	British and Australian	Range in yards
Calabria	about 1,200	about 2,400	33.3k–9.3k
Cape Spada	about 500	2,038	21k–17k
Cape Spartivento	677	about 1,300	34k–16k
Gavdos Island	629	36	31.7k–23.5k
First Sirte	140	about 580	35k–13.8k
Second Sirte	1,490	2,807	23k–6k
Pantelleria	3,371	about 3,400	22.4k–5.2k
% direct hits to shells fired	0.299%	0.111 %	

CONFIRMED NEAR-MISSES		
Calabria	*Alfieri, Freccia*	*Neptune* (two times), *Sydney, Nubian, Hereward*
Cape Spada	–	*Havock*
Cape Spartivento	*Bolzano, Libeccio*	*Manchester*
Gavdos Island	–	*Orion, Gloucester, Ajax, Perth*
First Sirte	–	*Kipling, Nizam*
Second Sirte	*Gorizia*	*Euryalus, Cleopatra, Penelope, Havock, Lively, Lance, Sikh, Zulu, Legion*
Pantelleria	–	*Cairo* (7 shorts), *Marne, Matchless*

Instances of misfires, drill errors, guns not being ready, mechanical breakdown, etc. were evenly balanced between the two sides. On 28 March 1941, *Veneto* lamented 11 misfires from expending 92 15in shells (11.95 per cent). On 24 May 1941, the German battleship *Bismarck* recorded 15 per cent and the British *Prince of Wales*, 25 per cent. Three days later, during the destruction of *Bismarck*, between 25,000 and 2,200yds, about 200 of the 2.876 rounds fired by the British against this stationary target misfired. Different guns and ranges, of course, but the law of averages suggests that some unexamined assumptions about Italian naval gunnery during World War II invite differing conclusions to those of popular and even scholarly accounts, which are too often based on biased accounts written soon after the end of the war by some German admirals, including Dönitz and Eberhard Weichold (liaison officer with the RM between 1940 and 1943), during their captivity.

Colombo (Ceylon), 1 June 1945. The destroyer *Carabiniere*. When war against Japan was declared by Rome on 15 July 1945, *Carabiniere* was still sailing with the Eastern Fleet as a plane guard destroyer for search and rescue purposes. (AC)

RM pattern size spreads for line and range appeared to be effective. Cunningham admitted, in July 1941, in a secret memorandum to the Admiralty: 'the enemy's range accuracy in long range day action has on occasions been better than ours' and 'The only satisfactory day action ... was H.M.A.S. *Sydney* v. *Colleoni*'.

The two navies historically had two different doctrines: the RN traditionally favoured rate of fire despite the Admiralty's instructions which stated: 'In action, there is a grave temptation for a director layer to "get rid of the salvo", and it is most desirable to educate all director personnel that Accuracy is more important than Speed'. In a sense then, the Regia Marina's gunnery was, thus, more truly British than the Royal Navy's as the Italian rule of thumb was for a slower, but more accurate, firing cycle.

Other aspects of the RM's performance, other than gunnery, confirm the reliability of the fleet's machinery and its ability to reach the real projected (not the ones claimed by *Jane's*) speed.

Underwater protection was excellent for the Littorios, which survived six torpedoes. The heavy and the second generation of the light cruisers sustained seven torpedo hits without sinking. The loss of *Trento* was caused by a second torpedo hit which detonated an 8in magazine, while the crippling of *Cavour* and *Pola* was caused by magnetic pistols exploding under the hull, where only the Yamatos had protection. However, the first generation 5,000t Condottieri cruisers proved to be no better than the 5,600t British Didos: two torpedoes each sank *Colleoni, Diaz, Di Giussano, Da Barbiano* and *Bande Nere*.

Armour was little tested in battle, but *Cesare, Bolzano, Bande Nere, Montecuccoli* and *Eugenio* dealt well with the shells they were forced to endure.

The Regia Marina was not a well-balanced navy due to the lack of carriers. Its core, the battleships, had limits, some known and others unsuspected. It was obvious that the modernized Cavours and Duilios were not a match for the Nelsons or the modern KGVs (King George V class). Not by chance the British considered them a sort of battlecruiser.

The only true Italian battleships were the Littorios. It was not known that the 32cm (12.6in) AP shell in fact had the highest-piercing qualities expected from its excellent design, steel and thick walls, but its blast and destructive power was relatively weak because its TNT burster was only 14lb compared to the 39.6lb of the old Italian 12in shell, not to mention the modern British 15in AP shell (48lb). At Jutland, *Warspite* was hit (but her armour not pierced) by 15 German shells between 11 and 12in. The Italian 12.6in shell (1,157lb compared to the old 12in 997lb) was able to pierce the armour deck, but with little effect. The Ballistic Research Laboratory of Fort Halstead, and the Royal Gunpowder Factory at Waltham Abbey, criticized the Italian AP fuses, but based on the numbers of the duds they were better than the Germans and comparable to the British.

Lack of effective radar sets until May 1942 was, of course, a further handicap at night and for air warning. But it did not affect, until the Italian Armistice, fire-control, as the clear sky of the Mediterranean allowed Italian rangefinders and director systems to work well while contemporary RN low-angle surface fire control radar sets had a range of 24,000yds at best.

In conclusion, the complete picture of the different strategies of the Regia Marina and the Royal Navy is often misunderstood. Italian strategy was a subtle and multilateral approach led by political and economic long-term motives. Given the dire economic situation Italy faced, it was a political miracle to have fought and resisted so tenaciously under the circumstances, and La Squadra, by far the most important part of the Italian forces, made a substantial difference.

FURTHER READING

Primary Sources

Archive Centre, Churchill College, Cambridge. Committee Report on the Accuracy of Naval Guns, Feb. 1944, Oliver Papers, OLVR 2/7

Archivio dell'Ufficio Storico della Marina Militare (AUSMM), Rome, Italy

Fondo Comandi navali complessi

Fondo Commissione d'inchiesta speciale, Navi

Fondo Commissione d'inchiesta speciale, Personale

Fondo Considerazioni e relazioni su avvenimenti della Seconda Guerra Mondiale

Fondo Promemoria di Supermarina

Fondo Scontri navali e operazioni di guerra

Fondo Squadra Navale 1 e 2

Fondo Supermarina-Comando Supremo

Fondo Supermarina, Diari. Titolario S10

Fondo Supermarina-Santa Rosa

The National Archives (TNA), Kew Garden, Surrey, UK

ADM 199/396, '18th Cruiser Squadron, War Diary 1.3.1940–31.12.1940'

ADM 199/897, Reports of Proceedings by HMS *Aurora*

ADM 199/1048, 'Action off Calabria, 9th July 1940'

ADM 199/2378, 'Preliminary Narrative of the War at Sea', 1946

ADM 205/10, Note by H.R.M. to Pound, 9 December 1941

ADM 223/89, Report of Medical Intelligence Centre

ADM 234/444, 'H.M. Ships Damaged or Sunk by Enemy Action 3 Sept. 1939 to 2 Sept. 1945', 1952

Secondary Sources

'Admiral of the Fleet H.R.H. Philip', *After the Battle*, No. 7, 1975

Bagnasco, Erminio, 'Q&A', *World War Studies Quarterly*, Vol. 6, no.1/2009

Bagnasco, Erminio and De Toro Augusto, *The Littorio Class: Italy's Last and Largest Battleships 1937–1948*, NIP, Annapolis, Maryland, 2011

Bagnasco, Erminio and De Toro Augusto, *Italian Battleships: Conte di Cavour and Duilio Classes 1911–1956*, NIP, Annapolis, Maryland, 2021

Ballantyne, Iain, *Warspite*, Pen & Sword, Barnsley, 2000

Black, Jeremy, *Strategy and the Second World War*, Robinson, London, 2021

Carne, William (author), Carne, Mark (compiler), *The Making of a Royal Navy Officer*, Uniform Press Brighton, 2021

Cernuschi, Enrico, *Sea Power the Italian Way*, Ufficio Storico della Marina Militare, Rome, 2023

Churchill, W.S., *Step by Step*, Thornton Butterworth Ltd, London, 1939

Crawford, Kent R. and Mitiukov, Nicholas W., 'The British-Italian Performance in the Mediterranean from the Artillery Perspective', *History & Mathematics: Trends and Cycles*, 2014

Harker, Jack S., *Well Done Leander*, Collins, Auckland, 1971

Hatfield, George, *H.M.A.S. Perth 1939–1941*, Springwood, Faulconbridge, 2009

Hinsley, F.H., Thomas E.E., Ransom D.F.G. and Knight R.C., *British Intelligence in the Second World War,* Vol. 1, Cambridge University Press, Cambridge, 1979

Le Bailly, Louis, *The Man Around the Engine*, Kenneth Mason Ltd., Fareham, 1990

Marder, Arthur, 'The Royal Navy and the Ethiopian Crisis of 1935–1936', *American Historical Review*, 1969

McBride, Keith, 'Six-inch Guns in Pairs', *Warship 1997–1998*, Conway Maritime Press, London, 1997

Reynolds, David, *The Creation of the Anglo-American 1937–1941. A Study in Competitive Co-Operation,* University of North Carolina Press, Chapel Hill, 1982

Reynolds, David, *In Command of History. Churchill Fighting and Writing the Second World War*, Penguin, London, 2005

Roskill, Stephen, *H.M.S. Warspite. The Story of a Famous Battleship*, Collins, London, 1957

Roskill, Stephen, *Churchill & the Admirals*, Collins, London, 1977

Sadkovich, James, 'Rebuttal to Bagnasco Q&A', *Global War Studies Quarterly*, Vol. 7, no.1/2010

Salerno, M. Reynolds, *Vital Crossroads. Mediterranean Origins of the Second World War, 1935–1940*, Cornell University Press, Ithaca and London, 2002

Schmidt, Rudi*, Achtung-Torpedo los!*, Bernhard & Graefe, Koblenz, 1991

Smith, Kevin, *Conflict over Convoys. Anglo-American Logistic Diplomacy in the Second World War*, Cambridge University Press, Cambridge, 1996

Sturtivan, Ray, *The Swordfish Story*, Arms and Armour, London, 1993

The Australian War Memorial, Rex Cooper Diary, Accession Number AWM2018.20.22. Collection Number PR01950

Winter 1940–41. The crew of the heavy cruiser *Zara*. (AC)

INDEX

Note: Page locators in **bold** refer to captions, plates and pictures.